ONE HUNDRED GOODBYES

On Addiction, Heartache, Grief, and Love

Dearest reader —
you are so loved ♡

Dr. Nicole Anders

ISBN: 978-19-5-036774-0

Published by

If you are interested in publishing through Lifestyle
Entrepreneurs Press, write to:
Publishing@LifestyleEntrepreneursPress.com

Publications or foreign rights acquisition of our catalog books.
Learn More: *www.LifestyleEntrepreneursPress.com*

Printed in the USA

For Cody
May my love supersede time,
space, and dimension.
I love you all ways, always.

For every beautiful soul struggling with addiction – You are not alone. You are loved. You are enough. You are worthy of this life. There is support available for you. Please do not let your shame cause you to suffer in silence. There is nothing to be ashamed of.

For all those who love someone who has lost their battle to this heartbreaking disease – I hope that my words can help your healing hearts if only for a moment. We are not alone in our grief.

INTRODUCTION

Grief is inescapable in this human experience, and yet it often feels like one of the single most isolating events a person can go through.

I've been here before; I'm no stranger to heartache in my mere 30 years. But every time it leaves me breathless, gut-wrenched, and heartbroken in an uncharacteristic solitude.

Have you, too, been here before?

As a clinical psychologist, I am self-aware of my coping mechanisms, both healthy and less so. I understand that "these things take time" and sometimes the only thing to do is nothing at all. I know all of the common platitudes as well as the psychobabble speak, and still, I find myself gasping for air.

Cody was my little brother, and it's not hyperbole when I say that he was one of my best friends—a soulmate of a sibling in many ways. Losing him took me to my knees. It's that split second when you get the phone call that just buckles you. You've been there. When all you want to do is rewind time and unhear the tragic news. When you beg and plead with a God you're not sure you even believe in. Please, please, please, let this not be real. Please.

I'm a psychologist by trade, yogi by heart, and writer by soul. A passion I let fall to the wayside because, as you know, sometimes saying it out loud or writing it down just makes it too goddamn real.

But, as a year slowly and quickly marched by, I realized I couldn't numb or distract anymore. I needed something, anything to help me move through it.

I created a project, dedicating 100 days to 100 contemplations, to come up with 100 writings, all for you, Cody, all for you. When we believe that words are failing us, it is then that we should do the work to search deeper, reflect longer, and find the poetry within us to come out of isolation.

To connect to everyone and anyone who has ever lost someone. With my project, and my words, I have already begun to find solace in the community that is grief.

And so it is.

....

....

I wrote that short piece on April 1, 2019. Like most of my writing, words and ideas bounce around in my head for a while, until I find a moment to spit them out onto my iPhone in the notes app. It's rather sophisticated, I know. I had been dreading that day, the first anniversary of losing Cody. I wanted to celebrate his life; I really wanted to be in a place of celebration, but I couldn't find it within me. I just felt haunted by the 365 days that had passed without him, knowing that marking one year only meant more years to come.

I was a new mom and a newlywed, with a freshly broken heart. I had spent most of the first year without him in a daze or in a distraction. Less than three months after he died, my son was born prematurely. On a casual Sunday afternoon, my husband and I raced to the hospital, only for me to undergo a cesarean a few days later. We spent one week in the NICU, and several months at home in a sleepless stupor. Oh, and me with the hormones. I can't forget about how those little regulatory substances did anything but regulate me postpartum. Then, when my son was just 73 days old, my mother-in-law died. Our family rushed up to Canada to sit at her bedside as she passed away, after losing her 34-year battle with cancer. After five weeks in Canada, we returned home, I returned to work, and my husband was deployed, for lack of a better term. He is not enlisted in the military, but the field he is in causes him to be away for many weeks at a time, sometimes with poor means of communication. In some respects, it's comparable to a military deployment. We definitely go through very similar motions.

So there you have it... A year of chaos, fear, and pain, sprinkled in with the most joy I have ever felt. As the one-year anniversary fast approached, I sat with myself. I took a long, deep look at my emotional body and realized just how unprocessed and unhealed my grief was. Time wasn't healing this wound. I felt everything, all at once, as if every day was the day I lost my brother all over again. Even in happy moments with my son, I found myself in confusing tears. My joy had become bittersweet. I was angry, infuriated. I was absolutely devastated. I was searching for something to help me.

I had been searching for a therapist I could connect with, not finding the right match. As strongly as I believe in psychotherapy, I do not believe in settling for a therapist just because they take your insurance or because their office is down the street from you. If you truly want to do the work, finding the right healer is nearly as important as choosing who you'd like to marry. And I didn't have the energy to keep going on bad dates. I knew what I needed. I had all of the clinical knowledge, but I couldn't sit on both sides of the couch at the same time.

So I asked myself, *If you were your patient, what would you say?* I would tell myself that it was time to face my heartache. That I needed to talk about it, even if it was painful. I needed to go back to the memories and moments that haunted me. I needed to let each wave of emotion wash over me, in its own timing, letting go of the illusions of control. And suddenly, it felt simple. I needed to get back to pen and paper, get back to finding the poetry to express my pain and to express my acceptance.

When I was four years old, I was asked what I wanted to be when I grew up. "I want to write books," I said. I've found comfort and catharsis in words. Sitting in front of a screen, taking a deep breath, and finding the perfect synonym; this calms me. I love to read and write and find a deep human connection in the sport. Turning to writing now seemed so obvious to me.

I called one of my best friends one sunny Vegas afternoon in March 2019. "I have an idea," I explained. "I want to write letters to Cody; maybe one hundred would be a good goal. I just need to force myself to write, and just let whatever shows up, show up. Unedited. Raw. Without a filter."

She encouraged my idea. "Post them! I want to read them. I love your writing." And with that conversation, the idea was born. I sat down and spoke to Cody.

The hundred posts took me nearly one year. The second year I spent without him was quite opposite of the first. I was incredibly intentional in my healing. I felt very connected to him as I let myself dive into each stage of grief, out of order, and then back around again. I slowed down, I felt my heart, I used my alone time to meditate on the pain. I shared my experience, and it started a domino effect. I found connection. I felt comforted by others. I felt my words comfort others. My healing project blossomed and bloomed into a platform of love, one that continues to expand and grow in ways I could have never predicted.

One hundred posts could never encapsulate the depth of my grief. One hundred posts did not magically take the pain away. Just the other night I felt such a longing for Cody that I sobbed myself to sleep, being held by a loving and patient husband who knows that sometimes I just need to let it out. One hundred posts will never be enough, but they certainly are meaningful. I look back on the journey and truly feel the experience of both writing and sharing them has healed me more than I thought possible.

I share them now with you, dear reader, along with five chapters on grief, one dedicated to each stage. Knowing that the stages are anything but chronological. Knowing that despite my clinical psychology background, I am simply one human, hopefully connecting to another through the emotions embodied in these pages. Knowing that we are never alone, even when it feels like we are the first and only person to experience our pains.

Close your eyes, take a deep breath, allow your heart to receive my love.

Love, Nicole
April 1, 2020

A MESSAGE TO MY READER

Though I am a licensed clinical psychologist, I would like to note that this book is not prescriptive; it is not meant to be used as a self-help guide, and it is definitely not meant as a substitute for therapy. If you are finding yourself struggling with mental health issues or difficulties controlling substance use, please reach out to someone. I am constantly humbled by the community of healers and helpers who are ready to step up with love. I am certain there is someone out there who is the right fit to help you. Please find my website in the ABOUT THE AUTHOR section at the end of this book and feel free to connect with me if you need help finding resources in your area.

In this memoir, you will read the letters I wrote and dedicated to my younger brother, Cody. The posts, starting at one and ending at one hundred, are in chronological order. They do not follow a sequence of steps or a perfect flow through the stages of grief. These are simply my personal thoughts, emotions, and experiences as I sat through the sorrows of losing Cody.

I have also included five brief chapters, weaved in throughout the hundred posts. Each chapter describes one of the original five stages of grief: Denial, Anger, Bargaining, Depression, and Acceptance. These five stages were initially identified by Elisabeth Kubler-Ross and David Kessler. David has since written on and explored a sixth stage of grief in his book *Finding Meaning*, which I highly, highly recommend. The stages are listed in order, but as you will plainly see, they are not experienced in this order. They are scattered. For me personally, I find comfort in identifying myself throughout the stages but in no way do I feel boxed in. I assure that Kubler Ross and Kessler's work was never meant to make anyone feel labeled or boxed in.

Thank you for allowing me to share my pain with you, for I believe that grief needs to be witnessed. In the truest meaning of the phrase, Namaste.

ONE.

One year ago, you took your last breath. From what I understand, your breathing slowed down and your heart decreased in speed until its final beat. I imagine it was peaceful, and I tell myself that it was a quick and painless slip from euphoria into death.

It still doesn't feel real. As is typical in grief, I have a what-if loop constantly playing in my mind. Begging the world to take me back to a moment in time where we could go left, instead of right. Cursing at a God that I don't think I believe in. Asking the Universe for a sign, any sign to help me understand what happens next. Where do we go after our last breath? Where did you go after yours?

I've been trying to find a path to healing. Pulling strings left and right from therapy to yoga, and everything in-between. I remember when I first found out that you died, one of the things I said was, "I can't, I can't go through this, I don't want to do this again." I was remembering how many, many years it took me to feel like I could even breathe again after our Mom died. I was remembering how long it took for me to talk about Mom without the intensity of sadness rushing through my veins. I was remembering that I only just started feeling whole again. I was remembering that going through losing Mom was only just barely tolerable, because we were in it together. "I can't go through this...." I was pleading to not go through the grieving process, and yet here I am.

TWO.

I spent yesterday reflecting on who you were and what you meant to everyone. I listened to our mutual friends share stories about you. It felt good to laugh, and cry, and to hear how your life touched those who knew you, those who loved you.

One incredibly impactful conversation I had was about compassion. One of my best friends said, "He helps me every day to be a little bit more empathetic, kind, and caring to people that I used to think didn't deserve it. For me that's his legacy and I'll carry him forever." She put to words how I feel, too.

There is so much stigma around addiction and mental health. I find that we other-ize people, in order not to see that their humanness is akin to ours. The homeless man on the street corner, the woman with a different skin color, the violent neighbor, the kid down the street who smokes pot. We recognize that they are just like us, but, out of fear, we quickly shift and decide that they are "nothing like us." To prove it, and to quell our fears, we ostracize, we push away, we judge and blame and assume. We look at the man using heroin with disgust, when our addiction to our phones can be just as harmful. We look at the woman who drinks too much as less-than, when our materialism is just as ugly. We other-ize. I other-ize.

Your legacy has taught me not to other-ize. The people who don't appear to deserve compassion are also somebody's child, somebody's sibling. They are somebody's somebody. They are somebody. My heart has forever shifted.

THREE.

I listened to a video from Oprah's *Super Soul Sunday* series
with Gary Zukav on multi-sensory perception. He speaks
about the soul, and his explanation of the difference
between a personality and a soul is incredibly impactful. He explains that we are personalities, here in our
earth-bodies, and that our experience is a school full of
lessons. He describes how our soul is here before we are
born into the physical realm and stays until much after
our death. He encourages us to challenge the perspective
of our personalities. When we feel trauma and suffering,
pain and loss. When we are in anguish and in deep grief,
instead of viewing the loss as a tragedy, we must shift
into the perspective of the soul. Souls choose when to
enter into the earth-school and when to leave. Believing
this, and living by this, we can find gratitude for the

opportunity to be gifted experience with each soul (and each personality) we encounter.

Sometimes when I find myself in the belief that there is a realm beyond this one, my science-mind taunts me and says, "What proof do you have?" I become doubtful. But my heart answers, "Proof I have not, and perhaps it is all a big lie, but it's the most beautiful lie I've ever heard, and I choose to believe." I choose to believe that our souls spent 27 and a half years loving each other in this earth-school and I promise to try and shift my perspective, to sit with the beauty of the all of the gifts. To sit with the beauty of loving your soul, and having the opportunity to be siblings in this school. My soul honors your soul.

FOUR.

My heart is just broken, I feel exhausted and hungover from emotion. My brain feels foggy and this week I've been staring at the computer screen in front of me, knowing what I need to do, mentally instructing my fingers to type, but coming up short. Grief has stripped me of energy and motivation. Grief has turned simple day to day tasks into long and arduous projects. I catch myself gazing off into space, eyes glazed over, desperately trying to reorient myself. Losing you has had me questioning everything, at times wondering why it all even matters.

My patients sometimes forget that I'm human too. Yesterday, I led a group therapy session for women who have survived sexual trauma. I approach the group in a process-oriented manner, holding space for others and guiding them toward insight. It's one of my favorite groups that I run.

When they ask me personal questions, I sometimes chuckle at the perspectives of me that their comments imply. "Do you ever wear a mask, Dr. Anders? Do you ever fake a smile too?" They are inquisitive. I reply, "I am only human after all." Little do they know, the smile that accompanies the reply is probably one of those smiles they're asking about. I am only human after all.

FIVE.

We decided it's time to sell your car. The leather interior still smells like you, even after all these months. Logically I know it's just a car, but I'm having a hard time letting it go. Positing it online and trying to put a price on four wheels and a grey body, slapped together with the Mercedes logo. Your car is where we danced and sang along to Fetty Wap, pretending to know all the lyrics. It drove us to lunch at that Hawaiian spot near my work, the one time when we argued, but moments later apologized. We never stayed angry for long. It drove you to visit me on the beach that summer's day, a few months before your passing. You sat in over an hour of California traffic before getting to me, only to spend a few moments together; a hug from your big sister was worth the traffic you said... Someone will come and look at your car and try to haggle down a few hundred dollars, as is usual with car sales.

It doesn't hold the same value to them as it does to me. They will be unable to recognize that when they drive away with your car, it will be one more piece of life without you. Loss happens all at once, and then piece by piece.... I think I'll just go for one last drive.

SIX.

Sometimes I just can't find the words. And when I do, I feel they barely do justice to my internal world. Ironic, isn't it? I started a writing project, only to feel like words aren't enough. But words are necessary, they are a piece of our connection to others. Song lyrics, poetry, Instagram posts. My words help you find your own. Your words fit perfectly for me.

I read a poem that Oprah posted, commenting on her own loss. Her posting fit perfectly for me. And yet, her posting was of another's words. A poem by Henry Scott-Holland. His words fit perfectly for her. And so it goes.

"Death is nothing at all.
It does not count.
I have only slipped away into the next room.
Nothing has happened.

Everything remains exactly as it was.

I am I, and you are you,

and the old life that we lived so fondly together is untouched, unchanged.

Whatever we were to each other, that we are still.

Call me by the old familiar name.

Speak of me in the easy way which you always used.

Put no difference into your tone.

Wear no forced air of solemnity or sorrow.

Laugh as we always laughed at the little jokes that we enjoyed together.

Play, smile, think of me, pray for me.

Let my name be ever the household word that it always was.

Let it be spoken without an effort, without the ghost of a shadow upon it.

Life means all that it ever meant.

It is the same as it ever was.

There is absolute and unbroken continuity.

What is this death but a negligible accident?

Why should I be out of mind because I am out of sight?

I am but waiting for you, for an interval,

somewhere very near,

just round the corner.

All is well."

SEVEN.

There's this nasal spray called Narcan. When a person has overdosed on an opiate, the use of Narcan can reverse the depression of the central nervous system and save their life. In a world where we are facing an opiate epidemic, this spray is a miracle. It can give someone a second chance. It can give someone their life back. It can give a mother her child and child her parent. This nasal spray should be in every home, every hospital, every street corner. Some people, wonderful beautiful activists and advocates, are making this happen. Spread the word, spread the education. Spread the Narcan. I think it's wonderful. And, I fucking hate it. Where was the Narcan when you needed it? Where was someone, anyone, when you were all alone; accidentally overdosing, in the bathroom, alone. Where the fuck was the goddamn magic nasal spray. Fuck you, Narcan.

EIGHT.

I keep your ashes in a glass jar in a decorative box in my room. The ashes are white and a bit grainy, like sand with some crunched up shells.

I had the jar out on my bookshelf at first but it was too difficult to look at. To stare inside the glass jar and see your "remains," as they so fondly call it. It was too hard to stare at this jar of white sand and think that's all that's left of you.

How is it possible that what's in this little glass jar could encompass all that you were, all that you are. Your 6 foot 2 frame. A body that placed in fitness competition, winning trophies and medals. Your green eyes with a hint of honey in the middle, same color as mine. Your tiny teeth and slightly crooked smile.

I stare at the glass, filled with white sand, and know that it's not really you. The remains have nothing of value remaining. Some religions believe that cremation is not only to dispose of the body in this life, but also to usher the soul into the next world or its rebirth into the next life. I like that.

NINE.

I went out to dinner with some girlfriends the other night. It was a blast; a rendezvous of high heels, lipstick, and girly cocktails. Conversation was flowing and we chatted and gabbed away about this and that. A story was being told about something and someone, and it was asked, "Oh, so he's a junkie?" It took everything in me not to stop the conversation mid-sentence to educate about the ignorance of that word. To scold about the fact that when we throw around labels like "junkie" or "druggie" or anything else so blatantly derogatory we are only per-petuating the problem, perpetuating the shame.

I told myself, *"It's not worth making a scene and derailing the conversation, she doesn't mean any harm."* So I bit my tongue. I bit my tongue, and I'm sorry I did. I've been thinking about it for days now. I promise I won't bite my tongue again, if it's all I can do to honor you.

Language like "junkie" is just as cruel and misunderstood as any racial slur, or a comment about someone based on their outer appearance. Language like "junkie" tells me that addiction is so deeply misunderstood. Language like "junkie" is shaming; and the shame cycle, that's a dark spiral to go down.

I promise I won't bite my tongue again.

TEN.

Believe it or not, I was recently asked by one of your friends if you faked your own death. Absurd, I know. He even accused me of being in cahoots with you, having set up the worst April Fool's joke of all time. I was at first confused; what kind of insane theory was this? Then I felt angry and offended; how on earth could someone even think such a thing. And finally I felt saddened and full of compassion; this is the extent that denial can take us to. This is denial at work.

Denial. One of the stages of grief. Denial: the action of declaring something untrue. Denial, my friend and foe, how I wish I could believe you. How I wish you weren't telling my mind a fairytale. Oh how I just wish wish wish.

ELEVEN.

How long will I love you? As long as stars are above you.
And longer if I may.
  And longer if I may.

TWELVE.

I truly believe that addiction is culturally, vastly misunderstood. The "war on drugs" is political propaganda, full of scare-tactics and untruths. The war lives inside of each human-being who struggles with addiction. Each precious, unique, and worthy human-being who is hungry for something, desperately trying all the wrong ways to cope with the existence that ails us all.

In his book, *Balancing Heaven and Earth*, Robert A. Johnson writes, "Most of our neuroses come from hunger for the divine, a hunger that too often we try to fill in the wrong way. We drink alcohol, take drugs, or seek momentary highs through the accumulation of material possessions. All the manipulations of the outer world carry with them an unconscious hope of redeeming our lonely, isolated existence."

Where did you learn to fill your hunger with poison? Where does anyone learn to numb out the pain, the loneliness? What could I have done to help you feel less lonely, less hungry? Have you finally found your satiation and peace?

THIRTEEN.

Grief isn't about letting go of the past, it's about letting go of the future. The past is always yours. I keep my past with you safely nestled in my heart, a little treasure box of memories. The past is at times painful to reflect on, but it's ours. It will always be ours.

Grief is about letting go of the future. All of the hopes and dreams and visions that we grow to expect. I expected you to meet my son; I expected you to buy him fancy baby clothes and use a silly voice when you spoke to him. I expected you to heal, to overcome, to grow on to get married and have babies yourself. I expected us to take our children on family vacations to Mexico or Hawaii, and show them all of our favorite beaches, reminiscing about our own childhood adventures. I expected it all. I took for granted that it was bound to happen.

Grief is about letting go of the future. This is where I'm stuck. These thoughts bring stabbing pains into my already broken heart. This, for me, this is the thick of it.

FOURTEEN.

Sometimes, for a few split seconds, I forget that you're gone. My mind almost picks up the phone to find you on speed-dial. I miss our calls, our chats that could last hours. The late nights when we felt like no one else could understand us and all that we'd been through. We were a team. You and me. We consoled each other through loss, through breakups, through moves and changes, ups and downs, highs and lows. Where are you to console me now?

FIFTEEN.

There are moments of peace, you know. It's hard to see them because they are so few and far between, little flickers within the heartache. There are moments of peace and acceptance, when I realize it's all going to be alright. I convince myself that maybe it was all meant to be. A skeptic of faith and destiny at times, but at times a firm believer. Maybe it was all meant to be. Maybe you graced me with nearly 28 years of love and friendship and that was enough. Maybe that filled my cup in ways I am yet to discover. Maybe your time here was up. On to whatever is next. Maybe now, you are healed, out of pain, out of the deep suffering I didn't see or understand. Maybe, just maybe, everything is playing out exactly as it was meant to. When I dance with these thoughts, I find a few exhales of peace.

SIXTEEN.

I didn't write yesterday. It was one of those days that was just filled to the top with overwhelm. There wasn't time or space in my emotional world to focus on writing. I think sometimes we have to honor that. Honor that it's OK to put our grief away, just for a breath, a pause. It's OK at times to push it aside and say, "Not now, I'll come back to you later." It's OK. It's protective. Sometimes we just have to honor that.

SEVENTEEN.

16 years ago, on the 16th of April, mom died. Fuck cancer, right? For the longest time the trauma defined me. I self-identified as 'the girl who lost her mom' and everything about me somehow always looped and tied back to being a motherless daughter. It definitely defined you, too. We connected over this loss and in some ways it brought us closer and closer in siblinghood; traumatic bonding.

Losing her defined me, until it didn't. Until I spent countless hours on a therapy couch in deep self-exploration. Learning to shift the meaning of April 16th and our mom's death into something of resilience and meaning. The anniversary just passed and I thought of her, but it doesn't stab my heart anymore. It doesn't drop me to my knees and leave me tangled in darkness. Many, many years after her death, April 16th has lost its pain.

I guess what it all means is there's hope. There's hope that one day, maybe in 16 years, I won't feel this devastated, this angry and heartbroken. Maybe, in time, I'll think of memories with a fondness and a smile, just like I do with Mommy. Maybe there's hope, a light at the end of my grief tunnel. Maybe there's a light.

EIGHTEEN.

I told your story today. I realized afterwards that it was the first time I had ever said any of it out loud. My voice shook, but I got through it.

I told your story. The story of how you loved animals. The story of how you excelled in every sport you ever tried. The story of how you binge-watched all the cheesy TV dramas with me.

The story I told was about a kind and sensitive human-being, in a lot of emotional pain. I shared your journey from a lens of compassion; even more compassion than I was ever able to show you when you were here. I shared the story that behind the addiction, you were a beautiful and selfless man. This is the story I will always remember.

NINETEEN.

They ask me if I still think about you.
Only all the time.

TWENTY.

I look back on all the memories, all the potential forks in the roads that led to today, but could have led elsewhere. I have the fantasy that I could have saved you, someone could have saved you, you could have saved yourself. I try not to get down on myself, but sometimes I lose the internal struggle and raise my white flag to the inner critic who tells me I should have known, I should have done something different.

At times I am filled with regret. I regret all of the nights we drank alcohol together. The margaritas in Mexico, the shots in Vegas. I regret smoking joints with you, back in high school, behind our school, on the trail near the train tracks. I regret the time we went to a rave and took MDMA. I regret any moment where I participated in normalizing substance use for you, even if we were just a couple of kids, experimenting with it all. I regret that we live in a culture where it's seen as developmentally normal, making it easier to hide behind, and harder to recognize when a problem exists.

I battle with these memories. I once looked back on them as 'good times, where fun was had' but now I am filled with regret. If I could have saved you, I would have. I'm sorry.

Denial

If I'm being honest, it still doesn't feel real.

"Your mind loves you." This is something I say to my patients all the time. Your mind loves you; this is why it blocks out painful memories, why it creates distorted thoughts, why it lies to you and tells you the truth is not real. Every person who has ever sat in my office and shared their innermost thoughts and feelings with me has become vulnerable, opening up about the persistent thoughts that haunt and pain them. Our minds are powerful. Scientists have barely scratched the surface when it comes to the mind, knowing only that we use a mere percentage of its capacities.

Most of us have a love-hate relationship with our minds. Knowing its problem-solving abilities or creative ways can allow us great success and joy. Knowing its cognitive distortions and habit of perseverating can cause us great sadness. When a patient walks into my office, I frequently inquire about the relationship they have with their mind and their thoughts. Many patients tell me, "I want to change my thoughts. I feel stuck here." This is a worthy and noble therapy goal, something realistic to accomplish even.

The first step, I believe, is to recognize that your mind loves you. It's a silly sentence that interns and patients alike tend to giggle at. It may be a very confusing sentence as well, when most of us believe that our minds and our thoughts are what clutch us in depression and anxiety. But, rest assured, your mind loves you. And everything it does, it does from a place of love and protection. Your mind has the best of intentions.

"How can this be?" I am often asked. "What is loving about repeating a self-blaming thought, keeping me up at night? What is kind about denying the facts of a traumatic event, or better yet, forgetting them entirely?"

Your mind loves you; hence, we enter into denial. For many people, denial is a raw and primary experience of grief. Of course, I would like to reiterate what Elizabeth Kubler-Ross and David Kessler (authors and founders of grief's five stages) have written in their works: These stages are not prescriptive. They are not chronological. They don't have a timeline that makes sense. Nonetheless, denial tends to be one that we experience from the get-go.

Our mind feels overwhelmed by the news. Our brain feels scrambled, and we often lose touch with reality. *No, this can't be. No. No. No.* It's too much, too difficult, too painful. So our beautiful, loving mind rejects it. Your mind does not want you to feel the agony and pain that comes along with the new reality. Sometimes we even go into detective mode, trying very hard to find proof of the contrary. To find proof that this is, in fact, a lie. *This can't be real.* We fill in the blanks, searching incessantly and often manically to prove to ourselves and others. Denial is the exact opposite of acceptance.

....

....

It was a Sunday, the first of April. A day for fools. I was 22 weeks pregnant. I had been having strange dreams and nightmares throughout my pregnancy. Kris, my husband, will recount the nights I woke him up as I tossed and turned with my growing belly.

It must have been around two o'clock in the morning—I actually never checked the clock—and I sprung up from my bed. I sat right up, tall. "What's happening?" I said aloud to my sleeping husband. "What's happening?" He was dazed, used to middle-of-the-night wakeups, but nothing like this. Normally I would grab his arm from a nightmare, he would put his hand on my back, and I would fall quietly back asleep. This morning, in the wee hours, I was completely awake, in panic. I still cannot explain the feeling I had; it was unlike anything I've ever felt.

"What do you mean? Nothing is happening," he replied, later admitting how worried he was. I sprung up, grabbed my robe, and charged downstairs. Turning on all of the lights in the house, room by room, checking for something. I remember it still. I felt frantic. What was I looking for? The door was locked, I assured. There was no one in sight. I turned the lights off and retreated back to bed. "What's happening, Nicole? Are you OK?" Kris asked.

Still dazed, I replied, "I don't know. I just feel like something is happening."

"Everything is fine. Go back to bed." So I did. I couldn't place it, this bizarre, panicked feeling. My mind loved me, as it always does, and decided to convince myself it was all in my head. *Nothing is wrong*, I repeated to myself. *The energy you are feeling, it's not real.* I laid down and easily drifted back to sleep.

We awoke several hours later. Nothing unusual. Nothing strange. I had actually forgotten about this wake-up until days later when Kris reminded me of the strange timing of it all. I walked downstairs, hand on my belly, in the same robe, with a much calmer energy. Kris was making breakfast—pancakes. My mind had protected me by completely forgetting about the experience. It happened to be Easter Sunday, so I texted with my family in Canada. We wished we were together and sent loving messages. The day continued on as normal.

Kris and I wanted to go for a hike that day. We drove out to Boulder City, Nevada and decided to hike through the tunnels on the edge of Lake Mead. It was incredibly hot in the desert that morning, and carrying the extra baby weight slowed me down. But I was happy. I was enjoying my Sunday. I was exercising and having great conversation with husband as we trotted along. Nothing out of the ordinary.

We returned home, and I sat on a wooden stool in the kitchen, listening to country music as my husband chopped vegetables, cooking our meal. Kris does not like country music, which I jokingly find to be one of his worst qualities. My stepmother, Julie, and her two sons love country music. So, on that evening, April first of 2018, I decided to call them with the intention of getting them to egg Kris on and poke fun at his lack of musical taste.

I phoned using FaceTime, as I always do. My dad answered. He was sitting in a dark room. He was emotionless and numb, but I didn't notice. "Hi, Dad. Where's Julie?" I asked, in a high-energy, upbeat mood. There was some silence. I was still clueless. "Where is Kris?" he asked. "I am going to hang up and phone you. I need to talk to Kris." My heart sank, but I still didn't understand. *What is going on? This is strange. Why is he acting like this?* Thoughts of the worst-case scenario crept in. But my mind loved me and told me everything was fine. It chose to dismiss the clues. It refused to look at what was right in front of me.

My dad phoned back, and I answered. "Dad! What's going on!" I demanded.

He was calm and quiet. "Let me talk to Kris," he said. I handed my husband the phone. I stared at him, heart pounding and racing. Staring at his body language, his facial expressions, anything that could tell me what was going on.

He didn't say much on our end. He was mostly listening. Then he started to say, "OK…. OK…. OK…" as he nodded somberly.

"What's WRONG?!" I began to raise my voice. In a panic. My head was spinning. I couldn't think. My mind still loved me and tried very hard to come up with answers of what could be happening. Even though my heart and intuition knew exactly what had happened. *No. No. No. That's not what happened. Everything is OK.*

Kris handed me the phone. "Your father wants to talk to you, Nicole." I couldn't muscle the energy to take it from him.

"No," I refused. "What is happening, Kris? Please tell me. What is going on?"

He was calm. There was so much love in his eyes. "Nicole, take the phone. You really need to talk to your dad."

I burst into tears. Repeating the word "no," hundreds of times, I began pacing. I refused to take the phone. It's like my mind was still protecting me. *If you don't take the phone, you don't have to hear the news, and you can prolong this reality just a little bit more.*

I don't know how I got there, but I walked toward the stairs in our house. I sat down on the wooden floor. I was in hysterics at this point. I knew. "I can't. I can't do this again," I kept saying to Kris.

"You need to call your dad back," he insisted as he redialed the number. He handed me the phone. I wouldn't take it. He held the phone to my ear, and I finally grasped it.

"Nicoley?" my dad questioned, only hearing my sobs on the line. He calls me this as a name of endearment; he has since I was little. "He's not in pain anymore."

Those five words broke me. I was stunned silent. The sobbing stopped. I could not move. I could not think. I could not breathe. My mind and body were trying desperately to reject the news. Tears rushed down my face. I dropped the phone. Time stopped and spun all at once. My mind was scattered. *This isn't real. It can't be. This is not real. This can be undone somehow. We can go back in time. We can fix this. This can't be real.*

Denial: because your mind loves you.

....

....

Denial is the first stage, but then it comes back in waves, crashing over your sense of reality, then washing away. There are days when I almost forget that Cody is gone. My mind creates a story that he is somewhere, alive and well, just not here. It was easy to believe this, especially during the first few months, because it was actually quite common that I would go a week or two without speaking to him. My mind struggled to wrap itself around the concept of his death, his nonexistence. When one week turned into one month turned into one year; you have no choice but to lift out of denial. Two years later, however,

I still go to grab my phone and text him a joke or a meme or a song title.

Denial is the mind's way of coping. It feels over-whelmed and shocked. It's an active refusal. I read some-where that your mind experiences "disbelief aftershocks," which makes a lot of sense. There is an untangling, an unweaving that occurs. Grief happens first, all at once, and then bit by bit. The new reality can't possibly sink in all at once. When you are reminded of something but you can't share it with them, when you have a burning question that only they can answer, when you're at a family gathering and their seat is empty; It's in these moments that denial recognizes that she can no longer stay. Her job is to protect you, to help you ease into the shock of your new life, your new reality. She cannot stay long, but like a good mother, she holds you and loves you, and then gives you the space you need to grow on your own. Denial gifts you with time to adjust, especially when all you want is more time. She's effective and protective; you need her at first.

TWENTY-ONE.

I drove to work this morning appreciating the sunshine, the quietness of the early hour, the birds as they sang. I think motherhood has done this to me. Slowed me down. Or maybe all the yoga. I notice things with a bit more attention, more awareness. It's hard for me sometimes, to see the beauty in the world, the details and the little things. I strive to live in gratitude but I feel conflicted, confused even. Why weren't you able to see it that way? How was it that we lived in such different worlds. Where were the birds in your world? Had they lost their song? Where was the sunshine to warm you in your darkness.

I think about the final years of your life, the struggle it was for you to wake up in the morning, sometimes in the afternoon. The struggle it was to fall asleep. The struggle it was just to be. There were no birds for you, and that just breaks my heart.

TWENTY-TWO.

Dahlia is turning 18 this year, she's going off to college in the fall. New York City, the Big Apple. You would be so proud of her. Can you believe our baby sister is all grown up? We talk about you all the time, her and I. Just last night on the phone I told her how much talking to her reminds me of talking to you. You are both stubborn and passionate, intelligent and sarcastic. Remember when we found out we were getting a little sister? And we were told we could decide together what her middle name would be. We couldn't agree, and now she has two middle names... Sorry Dahlia. It's the little things that make your absence stand out the most. In some ways, all the good and celebratory moments are a bit tainted, because now there will always be something missing.

TWENTY-THREE.

I saw a video yesterday of my friend's brother playing with her 9-month-old. It was adorable. Her brother posts about his niece all the time and it just makes my heart burst with happiness. You can tell he's so proud to be an uncle and he loves his niece to pieces.

I remember when I told you I was pregnant. I had a plan of how to tell you but Oma spilled the beans early. You called me, "Nix, am I going to be an uncle?" I tried to pretend I didn't know what you were talking about but then I caved. "Yes! I wanted to tell you in person!" You were excited and thrilled! Your voice changed and I could tell you were beaming. We didn't know the gender at the time, you said, "I should probably move back to Vegas so I can help you take care of the baby." Even in your moments of deep pain, you found ways to be selfless.

When I watched the video of my friend's little brother playing with his niece, my heart burst with happiness and simultaneously broke at the fact that I will never have a video of you and Austin like that.... therein lies my deepest grief.

TWENTY-FOUR.

I gave a presentation about PTSD this morning on Nellis Air Force Base. I had to pause for a moment because I began to tear up. There was a young man in uniform who reminded me of you. Blonde hair, light eyes, and a crooked smile on a tall frame. Even something about his hair reminded me of yours. I took a pause and choked back emotion. For a split second I had an image of you in uniform.

I remember, right before you died, you were struggling to figure out just what to do with your life. What was the next step? We spoke several times, amidst your sobriety, about joining the military. You asked me what branch I thought you should join and we agreed the Air Force would have been a good fit. You would have looked good in uniform. I recognize now that you were looking for something, anything to give you stability, safety. I didn't realize how unstable and unsafe you felt.

God, I just wish so, so badly that I could have seen you in uniform. That you could have taken your sobriety to the next level and followed your dreams, accomplished your goals, and found your path here on this Earth. I just wish.

TWENTY-FIVE.

My husband asked me if I think that writing about you every day is helping me. He notices my deep sadness and I'm sure it hurts him to know there's nothing he can do to take away my pain.

Writing about you brings it all to the surface. It doesn't allow me to push my feelings under the rug. This project gives me a place to put everything out there, to contain my sometimes chaotic feelings of grief and loss. I know that even if I wasn't writing every day, you would still be on my mind. By writing, I've found something to do with the memories that pop up, the feelings that need to be sorted.

Writing about you every day keeps me connected to my grief, but it also helps me move through it. The alternative is to not write, to not think about you, to not talk about it. In some ways that might be an "easier" alternative, but I know healing is not done through ease. The only way out, is through.

TWENTY-SIX.

It's been a long day without you, my friend. And I'll tell you all about it when I see you again. We've come a long way from where we began. Oh, I'll tell you all about it when I see you again.

When I see you again.

TWENTY-SEVEN.

27. The number of birthdays you made it to. Oh what I would give to celebrate one more birthday with you, one more sunrise, one more laugh over something only we could ever understand, one more bad rap song on repeat; I never understood your taste in music.

Poetry and song lyrics always talk about "one more day," but if I could just have one more day, it wouldn't be enough.

I am so thankful that our final conversation ended with an I love you, especially because throughout those last few years it wasn't always the case. There were so many ups and downs. I'm so thankful for that final phone call just 30 hours before your death. If I could have just one more day I would tell you over and over and over again how much I love you. I'd say it over and over, and that would never be enough.

TWENTY-EIGHT.

Isn't it wild to think that opiates come from a flower? Originally anyways. A beautiful orange poppy, the root cause. Then of course we synthesize it; fuck you big pharma. And we distribute opiates to ease and "kill" pain, painkillers. More like people killers. So this once-upon-a-time poppy is now accessible to us all, overly accessible, binding to our opiate receptors and tricking the reward center of the brain into thinking we need more, more, MORE. Our logic knows we don't need the opiates but the reward center tells us otherwise. It tricks us, through out-of-this-world, stronger than anything imaginable cravings. It causes the brain to believe that opiates are now essential to survival.

Opiates became bigger than you, a unstoppable force.

So who wants to argue with me about choice? Or dare tell me that you should "just say no"? Fuck you and your choice. Fuck you and your misunderstanding. Fuck you all, and your judgments. Fuck you.

TWENTY-NINE.

I've been feeling angry lately, too angry to write because my head cannot contain the words in any coherent fashion. When I feel angry I become dismissive and my tongue becomes sharp. I feel a fire, burning inside, asking to be let out, wanting to burn it all down. Anger is one of grief's delightful stages. Do you hear the sarcasm? That's anger too.

I'm angry at the world, at those who let you down. Angry at myself for not being able to save you. Angry at all of the times I was unkind or judged you, even if I was just being your big sister. I'm angry at our parents, for not protecting you from yourself. Angry at your friends who knew about your pain and didn't tell me sooner. Angry at those who hurt you, harmed you, or introduced you to darkness. I'm angry at you, for your secrets, for not feeling safe enough to share them all with me, for your relapse. I'm angry at all of it, at everyone.

When I feel angry I want to throw things, scream and yell, smash a window or two. But instead, it's in my anger that I find silence. I'm stunted by this stage of grief, paralyzed, speechless. I want to yell, but what would I even say?

THIRTY.

My friend died. I received the news a few days ago and it's got me all shook up. Just like you, she was happy and kind, secretly hiding her pain. You never know the battle someone is fighting. You just never know. And even if you know, sometimes mental health feels impossible to work through. I say this as a clinical psychologist, feeling at times helpless in my own field of expertise. How do you save a life? How do you help someone who is struggling to help themselves? How do you help yourself?

As I feel the grief of losing my friend, my grief journey feels compounded. Not a setback, but a speed bump. I've been slowed down and tired, lost in drifting thoughts, sad.

When I think of death, I also think of life. In my slowing these past few days, I've noticed the green of the leaves, the song of the birds, the joy in my son's laughter. I've soaked in it a little more. I think that's the way to honor you, to honor her, to honor those who are no longer here. I think we should let our grief move us into deep appreciation for every breath. And so I breathe.

THIRTY-ONE.

I drive past places, or hear songs on the radio, and you instantly come into my mind. I reflect on our times together. The good times still sting. The hard times ache.

I remember when we went to lunch near my work on Friday afternoon. You paid for my lunch, always selfless and giving. We got to talking about my work with trauma and our own trauma of losing our mother. Then you said something I'll never forget. You said, "Nix, you have no idea what I've been through, though." And you said it with such an intonation that my heart stopped and I heard you, I heard what you were saying between the lines. I heard your pain and I heard your shame. "Cody, I can help you if you tell me. If you just tell me what happened I can help you." But you didn't, you couldn't you said.

To this day I wish I pressed more. What happened to you that made you hurt so badly, made you feel so alone, so ashamed, so in fear. Who hurt you? What did they do. What decisions did you make that ended you up in places you regret. Drugs and alcohol take you out of your body, a disconnection from reality. What reality did you so desperately need to leave? What darkness was lurking in your world.

THIRTY-TWO.

"We're all just walking each-other home" —Ram Dass

THIRTY-THREE.

I went to the gym tonight. Honestly it's the first time in years I've stepped foot into one. Remember when you used to make me go with you? Forcing me to do sit-ups properly. We would laugh and laugh as you "trained" me. Pretty sure the real ab workout was from those deep belly laughs.

The gym was quiet for a weeknight. I imagined you in every corner. You used to live in the gym. How else could you have won trophies in the Jay Cutler Classic. You were so incredibly dedicated. You lived and breathed workouts and weights. Those were some of your best days. Determined was an understatement.

As I moved from machine to machine tonight, I had that sinking feeling of nostalgia wash over me. I would do just about anything for a Cody Anders workout; Those dreaded workouts where I was literally dragging my feet to go with you. If you were here, I would go with you every single day, just to have those times back. Every single day.

THIRTY-FOUR.

Most days it still doesn't feel real. My mind plays tricks on me and I imagine you're somewhere, just not here. Somewhere in your house, safe and happy. Or maybe at the gym, pumping iron. Or maybe walking your dogs, Dakota and Monkey. Somewhere, alive and well. My mind tells me these things, just for a split second, to ease the nauseous feeling that comes with grief's reality.

"He's just on an extended vacation," my mind whispers to my heart. I imagine you body-surfing the waves like we did in Cabo, or cliff jumping China Walls in Hawaii. On vacation in the sun, laughing, in peace. Maybe, in some ways, it's not really a lie. Maybe, the truth is, you are somewhere happy and free, somewhere far away. I just wish you'd fly back to me.

THIRTY-FIVE.

Somewhere over the rainbow. Somewhere. I'm writing you from our hiking and camping adventure in Havasupai, Arizona. Sitting on top of a cliff overlooking Mooney Falls, staring at how the reflection of the sun creates a rainbow glow. When I come to beautiful places like this, I can't help but exhale some sadness, wishing you were here.

I remember when we were kids, Dad used to take us camping and boating. You were the one who was fearless, inspiring adventure in me, your big sister. You'd always jump off cliffs with a fancy back flip, or hold on tighter when we were tubing, screaming "FASTER!" Once upon a time you were the adventurous one. I can't help but wonder when that stopped.

Did you forget the feeling of waterfall spray on your face, or the high we would get from chasing each other up rocks and mountains. When did the blue waters and bright green foliage stop being enough to keep you breathing. When did the pain in your heart close you off to the breathtaking beauty this world has to offer?

I hope that somewhere over the rainbow, you too have a turquoise waterfall.

THIRTY-SIX.

I'm unsure what I believe about the afterlife. Does it exist? Is it a paradise up in the clouds with a man named God who rules us all? I highly doubt it. But I do tend to think, and maybe hopefully believe, that there is something beyond our time in these human bodies.

I met a woman last weekend in a training I was leading. She described herself as a spirit medium. I sat and spoke with her in a casual and impromptu fashion. Who am I to say that it's not all true? I find my curiosity is piqued with all of this. The tales and myths and theories of an afterlife, of the spirit world, of the next step. Recognizing that we don't really know, and won't know until we are there. If there is a there.

One thing the medium said to me is that our language is irrelevant. Call them spirits, ghosts, energies, angels; she feels that it's all the same and it's a waste to get caught up in semantics. She said that if you listen, if you pay attention, if you tune in, you can see them, feel them, and hear them. They'll flicker lights and send you signs, playing with the energies that we are more familiar with.

Could it be true? Could it be you that lights up my son's toys when no one is near them. Could it be you who blows the wind to send me messages, just exactly when I need them? Could it be you who gently nudges me to look at words and numbers that seem all too relevant for coincidence? Could it be you who, in the middle of the night, flashes rainbow lights outside of my car window when there's no light in sight? Am I looking for a self-fulfilling prophecy, or could it be you.

THIRTY-SEVEN.

Yesterday my patient smelled of cigarettes. He walked into my office and I noticed it immediately. It was a strong, awful stench. He's trying to quit, but is struggling. I had no judgment, but my nose did. As I spoke to him, exploring his inner most thoughts, I noticed myself drifting and feeling nostalgic with the smell. You used to reek of cigarette smoke. I say this now, lovingly.

In Jan 2018, during the last trip I saw you, I picked you up from the airport. I was newly pregnant and in my first trimester. It was a Thursday night, you were in your favorite leather jacket; the one I kept, it's hanging in my closet. You got into my car and like the bratty big sister I said, "Ew Code you stink! I don't want you smoking near me, it's awful." The pregnancy nose was making it worse than usual. I couldn't tolerate the smell.

I'm sorry for that moment. I'm sorry for that exchange. I'm so sorry for shaming you and your struggles with nicotine, with addiction. What I should have said was, "Cody you made it! I'm so happy to see you! I love you so much and I'm glad you're here to spend time with me." That's what I should have said. That's what I wish I said.

Please hear my apologies and know that if I would give anything to smell those cigarettes on your leather jacket as you enter into my car. I would do anything to crinkle my nose at the stench of tobacco and nicotine. I would do anything to be grossed out by that goddamn cigarette stench, if it meant having you back.

THIRTY-EIGHT.

When I'm busy I don't think about you. Or maybe I should more accurately say, I think about you less frequently; I'm still not sure a day has passed without thoughts of you. My packed schedule hasn't lately allowed time for long nostalgic pauses or sit-down moments of reflection and writing. Is it selfish of me to want to stay in that automatic state? Letting time slowly and quickly pass by all at once.

I thought about your voice the other day, wishing I hadn't deleted past voicemails from you. If I close my eyes in all the hustle and bustle of my days, I can still hear your voice. I still hear it clearly. I hear you saying my name. That auditory memory was once on the tip of my eardrum, living there day in and day out. Now, though, it takes me time to find it. I have to close my eyes and go there. It's no longer within a second's grasp.

My biggest fear is forgetting. As much as I want to get sucked into my daily to-do lists, avoiding the painful reality that you're no longer here, I also am simultaneously terrified that if I don't think of you constantly, your voice will slowly disappear. I can't let you disappear, but I can't sit in the agony of my grief every day, keeping the pain so fresh. What's the compromise? How do I hold your voice in my heart, in my head, yet not be dragged down by it.

THIRTY-NINE.

I went into the garage today, looking for some plastic bins to nicely fold and tuck away some of Austin's clothes. He's almost a year now, I just can't believe how simultaneously fast and slow time ticks by.

I stared at the corner of the garage where all of your things are in yellow and black bins, nicely labeled, moved from your storage unit into my home. I see the bins every day, sometimes in the background noise of my entering and exiting the garage. Sometimes I'm more aware of them and I tell myself that soon I'll go through them, *soon*.

I took a deep breath and opened one of the boxes, it was labeled "dress shirts." The clothes have been sitting here for over a year, but I picked up a shirt and brought it to my face. It smells like you. Somehow, it still does. I felt a ball in my throat and my eyes began to water and I put the shirt down, only to pick up another.

They all smell like you. I feel them, the fabric, the texture. I look at the fancy labels like Vince and Prada, knowing that this was part of the addiction. Hiding behind labels and brand names. I smell a few more pieces of clothing and change my mind about the entire undertaking. I can't do this. Not today. Not now. Not while it still smells like you, while you're still in those bins somehow.

I tuck the clothes away, put the lid on, and exhale, committing to keeping the bins a little longer. Unsure what I'm waiting for. Maybe I'm waiting for the smell to evaporate, or maybe I'm waiting to heal a little more. How long is too long to have these bins take up space in my heart.

FORTY.

I walked out of a presentation at work yesterday. My sweet and compassionate intern was presenting her dissertation on substance use. To be honest, I don't even exactly know what the topic of her presentation was, my mind started to jumble and I felt hot and dizzy as she began saying words like "prevalence of relapse" and "can result in death" and "do we need to treat this a different way?" I could only sit there for the first five minutes, staring at the PowerPoint with a racing heart, thinking of a gameplay to politely but quickly excuse myself from the room.

I feel torn about my decision to leave the room, to avoid feeling triggered in front of my peers. I know I couldn't sit there in tears, but I also feel ashamed that I couldn't tolerate the topic. She was speaking about change, educating about a better understanding, and yet, all I could think about were flashes of you, laying on the floor in a bathroom that I've never seen, alone, lifeless. What good would change do you now? Too little, too late.

My reaction wasn't abnormal, I know that. I did some self-talk and normalized my lingering hurt and the raw-ness of my grief. I know it was OK that I left the room, but it was also an in-your-face reminder of just how not OK I am. I guess I just expected more from myself. We hold ourselves to these standards of healing. Repeating things like "I should this" and "I should that." The lesson here is, I shouldn't anything, and it's OK to not be OK, even if you do all the work, use all the tools, read all the books. Even if you're a clinical psychologist specializing in trauma, helping others to heal, even then, it's OK not to be OK.

Anger

This chapter was the most difficult for me to write. I started it over and over again. I would write, take a pause from writing, then find any excuse not to sit down and write again. It was the chapter I most wanted to avoid. For me, at this stage in my life, anger is the emotion I actively try to evade. This is because I truly feel I have already spent enough of my lifetime being angry and I just don't want to be angry anymore. It has been very difficult for me to have a healthy relationship with this emotion. I have done so much inner work to not jump immediately to anger and rage.

I also had some doubts about writing this chapter. Anger is not flattering; it's not ladylike; it's not professional. I sat at the dinner table with my husband one night and insisted that I needed to delete this entire chapter and find a different approach to write about anger. I worried that *if my patients found out* or *if my boss read this chapter* or *if my family knew how I really felt*…they would all abandon me, fire me, not want to see me, turn on me, reject me, disown me. The list goes on. I told him that I thought it was too revealing, too raw. Immediately, as I said these words to him, I knew that I was feeling extra vulnerable with this topic, and that what I had written was probably exactly the story I needed to tell.

....
....

I have dealt with an "unacceptable" anger for most of my life. I put the quotations around the word unacceptable because I, now, finally, do not actually believe that my anger is unjustified, intolerable, or unacceptable. I was told that it was. For many, many years. Both through explicit and implicit messages. Until I spent years on the other side of the couch, as a patient, working through my own traumas, I truly believed the lies I was fed. I believed that my emotions were too big, too much, and entirely unwelcome. Most especially, I once believed that anger, for a woman, was unbecoming and improper.

I tried for many years to suppress my anger. Putting on a brave face in all social settings, only letting those closest to me see the rage within. It always pushed them away. That's the thing about repressed emotion; it bubbles and boils, and you try as hard as you can to stuff it down, but eventually the lid bursts off and it's uncontrollable. The anger turns into rage, aggression, and violence. Violence is absolutely intolerable and truly is unacceptable. It just never starts there.

What could you be so angry about? you might have asked, watching me grow up in a wealthy suburb of Vancouver, British Columbia. I am a highly educated Caucasian female who comes from an upper-middle-class family. I attended an expensive college-prep boarding school. I travelled the world. In many ways, I exude privilege, and I own it. But I've been angry all of my life. I've been angry ever since I can remember, and no one ever showed me how to express it in a healthy way. The Anders family (my father's side) and the Robbins family (my mother's side) are two families that have zero clue about healthy expressions of emotions. Zero.

I remember being very young, angry that my parents divorced. They divorced when I was only three years old. I have zero memories with my parents married. Growing up, I didn't understand why my parents had separate houses when most of friends' parents were together. I was unable to understand the complexity of adult relationships and I lacked the language to express any of it. I would fantasize about ways to bring them back together, only to become frustrated when my plans didn't work. Sometimes I even had thoughts that it was my fault. *Why did they divorce so shortly after having children? Was it us? Were we too much?* Confused and angry, I sometimes even directed that anger at myself, questioning my self-worth.

I remember being very angry at my mother for dying. I felt embarrassed to say that out loud for years, but in the mind of a 14 year old, it made sense. Of course, she never wanted to leave me. But the cards were dealt, and she lost. In my mind, she left me, and I was livid. I was angry at the God that she taught me to believe in. I decided to throw my Bible in the trash, never going back to the teachings of a "man" so cruel that he would take away my mother. I've never gone back to religion. I don't think I ever will.

I was angry at my father, for not seeing how badly I needed his love after my mother died. I now look back and see that he was doing the best he possibly could, with the resources he had, during a very difficult situation, raising two, young, grieving children. I was furious at him for not being able to read my mind, or read my heart. I was mad at him for not being my mother. For not being something he could never be. The expectations were unrealistic, but I held them anyways.

I was angry at my father's wife, my first stepmother, for not being my mother. For not being a mother to me at all. For giving me alcohol when I was 14 years old, right after my mom died, and telling me it would help me "feel better." She didn't know how to help me and my immense grief. She didn't realize my acting out was not a personal attack against her, but a serious cry for help. I was enraged with her for not loving me the way I needed to be loved. For losing her patience with my acting out and hitting me, giving me a bloody lip that I had to lie about. I felt abandoned when she did not protect me but instead, caused me to need protection. She has been the hardest one to forgive, but I now see that she was met with an impossible task, with two, very difficult, grieving teenagers that were not her own.

All of this anger, all of it, bubbled and surfaced within me before I even had my driver's license. I lived with anger and fury at the world. In true teenage form, I couldn't see past my own lens. I raged inside and had zero idea how to express it, other than to walk to the Walmart that was across the railroad tracks from my high school, buy a ten-dollar box of hair dye, and turn my blonde hair jet black. I even picked up smoking cigarettes for a few months. It was part of the image. It was a demonstration of how I felt inside. I had a lifetime full of pain, with no place to put it. It wasn't until a decade later that I finally began to sit with my emotions, including my anger, and piece through the debris.

I think about my anger and then I think about Cody. As an extrovert, I displaced my anger into acting out. I cursed at my high school teachers and took it upon myself to get into fist fights with other kids. I found a "valid reason" to lose my shit and let it out. Some examples that I remember were when I pushed a male classmate down the stairs at school because he had shoved my friend (his girlfriend at the time). Another time I slapped a classmate across the face because she said a snarky comment to me about "not being raised right."

It got to be so repetitive that I started to walk myself to the principal's office and confess my crimes immediately after they occurred. Looking back, I think it was my way of saying, "LOOK AT ME. I AM CRYING FOR FUCKING HELP."

But Cody was an introvert, and in many ways my stormy anger overtook the energy in our broken family. I found incredibly unhealthy outlets, and he just remained quiet. He bottled it up. He bottled it up some more. I was always in trouble while he watched from the sidelines. I have an image of him, one awful night, when I was maybe 16. I came home drunk after drinking too much flavored Smirnoff in the park with my friends, and got into a verbal altercation with my then-stepmother. I remember peering down the hallway as we exchanged words. Cody, only 14, was standing there in his doorway, in the dark, just watching, uncomfortable, afraid, and alone. That image is burned into my memory. I see it all the time. I see him, sad and confused; both of us wishing so badly that our mom was still alive and we were back in her arms.

I am still battling the distorted story that my anger and my teenage rage were somehow to blame for Cody not learning how to express his emotions. I've told myself the story that *if only I was not so difficult, taking all of the energy, somehow, he would have had more space to be seen.* Of course, this is untrue, but it still pops into my mind sometimes. I work diligently to challenge my automatic thoughts and find alternative stories to tell myself. *Just because you were a difficult teenager does not mean you were a bad person. You are not to blame. You were hurting, with no outlet.*

I suppose my outbursts finally worked though, and my father worked hard to find the right therapist to fit my needs. Someone I finally liked and didn't yell at, didn't sit in silence with, didn't tell to fuck off. I will never forget her; I saw her weekly for nearly two years from age 15 to 17, and she saved my life. She was the first person who tolerated my anger. She was the first person who let me rage and yell and scream and didn't run away. She didn't fire me as her patient. She didn't even judge me. She is the reason I decided to become a psychologist. She is the reason my path took a sharp turn down a much better life road. (I have spent years trying to track her down with no avail. So, Beth Helsley, of North Vancouver, if you are reading this, thank you from the bottom of my heart for being the guiding light that you were for me. Words cannot amount to the gratitude I have held for you for 15 years).

My anger, and all of my other emotions, finally had a place to be. Cody, on the other hand, presented a mask to the world that was unlike mine. Cody was calm, he was sensitive, he was loving and giving. Cody seemed fine. He didn't punch other students or swear at his teachers. Cody stood, down the hallway, in silence, just watching as I bulldozed my way through high school. Later, I found out that Cody found comfort in marijuana and other recreational substances. It broke my heart when I learned that he would go to school, almost daily, high on something. From pot to magic mushrooms to LSD. I think about this, and again, I feel angry. Angry at Cody for making these decisions. Angry at my father and ex-stepmother for not noticing. Angry at our boarding school and its teachers. Angry at myself for being too absorbed in my own pain. Who did not see the 15 year old high on acid, in class?! How did no one notice? HOW THE FUCK DID NO ONE NOTICE?!

....

....

When I allow myself to dip my toe into anger, I feel it immediately flow through me. It feels like it swallows me whole sometimes. I have had moments that I refer to as "rage blackouts," when I was so angry that I truly had no sense of logic or reason, my frontal lobes were shut down, and I quite literally felt as if I was drunk on the emotion, no filter, engaging in words and behaviors that I would later regret or even forget. When I dip my toe back into anger, I usually pull it right out, fearful that I could find myself in one of these blackouts again, even though I truly haven't had one for years.

Anger scares me; it causes me to explode. I believe that Cody's anger and pain scared him—and caused him to implode.

After high school, I attended college in Hawaii. Something about the Aloha spirit and being barefoot on the beach were the beginnings of my healing. My anger persisted though, showing up in relationships, in friendships, and with strangers alike. Graduate school moved me to Southern California, where I continued to grow and heal in many ways, but the rage within me still burned and showed itself from time to time, destroying more relationships on its path. My predoctoral internship moved me to Puerto Rico, where I planned to live happily ever after. Despite the sunshine and island vibes, that anger I held for the world just would not go away. "Wherever you go, there you are," the wise Jon Kabat-Zin speaks. And there I was, in the midst of unhealthy expressions of anger, like a tornado, destroying everything I thought I knew and wanted, putting an end to the fairytale I was writing. I was heartbroken to my core. This time, I was stuck on an island in the middle of the Caribbean, with very limited social connection, far away from best friends, family, and everything I knew. It was on this island that I was forced to sit with myself, alone, and feel.

I found my way back to the couch, to process these feelings in a safe space. I remember feeling embarrassed to tell my therapist how angry I was, holding back at first. I remember laying on my yoga mat in savasana, listening to my heart beating as tears of rage streamed down my face. I learned to control my breath and found my way to meditation. I practiced yoga daily and wrote in my journal nightly. I found a way to be alone but not lonely. I spent hours upon hours learning to love myself, with my anger, and in turn, calming my brain and body. Allowing myself to deactivate from a constant fight–flight–freeze state. Learning ways to self–soothe and gifting myself inner space, to think, slow down, and respond instead of react. It took the world to smack me down, strip me of all plans, and strand me on an island to do the work.

Meanwhile, while I was finally doing the work to heal my rage–filled heart, my brother was continuing to feel more alone and abandoned by me than ever. He saw all of my travels as escaping and running away, and he was angry that I had not taken him with me. I remember an argument we got into over the phone, time–zones away, where he said, "Nix, you left me here. You just left. How do you think that makes me feel?" That exchange still breaks my heart. Some days I am so angry at myself for leaving. Other days, I know that my staying would not have been the magic answer.

Cody was angry. I was angry. I think we had every right to be. But I had guidance, I had therapy, I had yoga, I had higher education, and the tools I needed to do the work. I had an outgoing personality that has never been afraid to use my voice to express my needs, for better or worse. The squeaky wheel gets the grease. Cody was too polite to ever squeak. He watched the tornado on the sidelines, turning to substances whenever he could not tolerate the emotions inside. I do not blame him, but there are days I am still so angry.

I am angry at the doctors who prescribed him oxyco-done for a back injury. I am angry at the medical system for not seeing how he would "doctor shop" when his prescription ran out. I am angry at his friends and ex-girlfriends for knowing about his addiction and never telling me. I am angry at his neighbors who clearly saw what was going on but did not reach out. I am angry at the dealers and the users and all of the people in the world that make illegal substances accessible to us. I am angry at Big Pharma and the pharmaceutical industry. I am angry at the researchers and scientists and chemists. I am angry at Cody. I am angry at his pain. I am angry at his darkness. I am angry at his secrets. I am angry at myself. I am angry at every single person who ever came into contact with Cody that didn't treat him with kindness. I am angry at everyone I've ever known to use words like *junkie* and *addict* and make tasteless jokes about drugs. I am pissed the fuck off at our culture and how it even encourages drinking and smoking pot "after a hard day." I am angry at this world for being so goddamn difficult and painful that we feel we need to escape ourselves. I am angry at the domino effect of everyone and everything that ever contributed to losing Cody. On my worst days, I am even angry at people who find the amazing courage, strength, and resilience to overcome addiction. How illogical is that?

Though, there is no logic in anger. Anger doesn't need to make sense; in fact, it never usually does. What I say when I am angry is never what I mean. Anger is a body-snatcher.

....

....

I said, "I've done the work." What I should have said was, "I'm still doing the work." The emotion of anger persists in being the most difficult emotion for me to sit with. I know that it is not a "bad" emotion and that it is simply a messenger. Anger says *something here is not right, something is unjust, something needs to be different*. This is the purpose anger serves in our lives. Anger can help you get your needs met. It can help you set a boundary and know when a boundary is being crossed. Anger can be powerful and full of life. It can be motivating. Anger can serve us too. Yes, it can haunt and plague us, but it can also serve and teach us.

I often teach my patients that anger is a secondary emotion. It is an emotion that lives on top of another emotion. "What is underneath your anger?" I will ask to explore. I look at my own pattern of anger and realize that when I am angry, I am usually scared. I am in fear. I am fearful of what might happen. I am afraid that I may be hurt or abandoned. I am scared that I may not have control and that will cause something awful. What is underneath?

....

....

I found it most difficult to post my angry letters to Cody. I found them unbecoming. I felt like other people would read them with disgust. That they might wonder how it was possible that someone like me, someone who is seen as compassionate, kind, and professional, could ever have moments of such inner rage.

Anger is the second stage of grief. Once the shock wears off, and you realize that your pleas will not work to bring them back, you find yourself engulfed in rage. *HOW DARE THIS BE SO?* I think in some ways this is a very necessary stage; it keeps you alive, and fueled, and motivated. However, you don't want to be stuck in either of two extremes when it comes to anger: being angry for too long, or alternatively, refusing to admit you're in anger.

We must give ourselves permission to feel the fire that comes with anger as it burns our insides. Covering up the fear and pain and moving you through. In her book, *Little Fires Everywhere*, Celeste Ng states, "Sometimes you need to scorch everything to the ground, and start over. After the burning, the soil is richer and new things can grow. People are like that, too. They start over. They find a way." Sometimes we need to feel angry and rage and burn and allow ourselves to be sucked into the flames to come out on the other side.

I have felt my anger, and I believe my soil is richer because of it.

FORTY-ONE.

All the breath in your lungs, is stronger than the tears in your eyes.

FORTY-TWO.

I went back to therapy last week, kicking and screaming. I didn't want to go. I created 1000 excuses in my head and came up with very legitimate reasons why I should cancel, up until a few minutes before the session. This might come as quite surprising as I'm a clinical psychologist by trade and I've been in and out of therapy since we were kids. But I just didn't want to go.

I didn't want to spend an uninterrupted hour in my emotions, in all the sadness and grief, all the pain and the devastation. As I sat there and told her about you, I was in tears. I couldn't look her in the eye, so I closed my eyes or stared at the ceiling as the space between our couches felt like it was closing in on me. At times I struggled to get out words, in-between choking on my tears, trying to catch a breath.

Ultimately I left feeling relieved. I left feeling heard and understood. I left feeling happy and proud of myself for making the time, for prioritizing myself. But now I'm just thinking of excuses for next time. How can I cancel the next session? Fantasizing about calling in sick and not going back, knowing that my better sense will gently force me to go. But damn, this is just so hard.

FORTY-THREE.

Dear universe: It's my birthday today. Another year around the sun. I have everything I could ever want and need. A beautiful family to love, abundant friends, endless joys… there's nothing I can think to wish for.

Of course if I had one wish, it would be to bring back those I love who have come and gone. Bring back my sweet mama, and my dear little brother.

My wishes aren't attainable in this lifetime, in this realm, of this I'm clear. But then, Universe, send me a sign. That's all I ask. Send me a sign today. A sign from above, or below, or in between. Send me a sign that there's something more, something to look forward to. Send me a sign that they're safe, out of pain, and immersed in love. Send me a sign, and today, I'll keep my eyes wide.

FORTY-FOUR.

"Alexa, play songs I like," was the request when I walked in the door from work yesterday, my birthday. The music played in the background and I thought nothing of it. I went upstairs to get ready for dinner with the parentals, they're in town visiting. After getting spruced up, I walked back down into the kitchen to pick up my son.

The exact second I walked into the kitchen, there you were. The exact second. The sign I had asked for only hours earlier. As clear as could be. I couldn't have planned for more cued timing. The song began and I smiled. I felt you. I knew. It was Mommy's song. It plays for me in times of need, it always plays. Across countries and oceans, this song finds me. And it found me again.

I looked at the clock that said 4:31. "For 31" here is your song, here is your sign. I cannot, will not, make this up.

Don't worry, about a thing, because every little thing, is gonna be alright.

And it is going to be alright.

FORTY-FIVE.

It's been a busy month. I still think about you almost every day, even if just for a nostalgic blink. Moments pass by and memories flood in. I haven't written you in a while, but you're always on my mind. Just because I am not writing, please know you're far from forgotten. I guess life without you has sort of morphed into something more tolerable, something at times I'm used to.

Other times, my tolerance is shattered and my body reminds me that you're gone. Gut wrenched, I have to catch my breath. When I first found out you were gone, I stopped breathing. I fell to my knees and for days and weeks and months there was nothing else I thought about. Someone told me that one day, several hours will pass without a thought of you, and then maybe even several days. This is healing, they said. This is the path it takes.

I think I'm at the point where an entire day can go by and you don't pop into my mind. It's rare. It's few and far, far between. But it has happened. And on those days, sometimes I don't want to write you. I guess, selfishly, I don't want to sit down and remember it all. To be honest, this scares me. Will there be a time when a week will go by without a thought of you? A month? I'm terrified to forget you. I know I never could.

I miss you in all the moments. The busy days and the slow. I miss you even when I'm not thinking about missing you.

FORTY-SIX.

I sat in therapy today and cried mascara down my cheeks. I sat and told her about my nightmares, about all the things that keep me up at night. I told her about the pain of missing you and the flashbacks I have in my mind... except, they're not flashbacks in the truest sense of the word.

A flashback is when the mind plays a trick on you, and for a brief moment, you flash to a time of the past, a traumatic encounter, a horrific image. Then, you flash again, back to reality, panicked and disoriented.

My flashbacks are exactly like this, except I flash to memories and moments I haven't actually seen. The mental images that flash before me are creations of my mind. I flash to you, laying on the bathroom floor, cold, alone, lifeless. Even though I've never actually seen the bathroom you died in. I flash to you using opiates and other drugs, in all sorts of dark, desperate, and scary situations that my mind draws up for me. I flash to you in pain somewhere, sad and crying, lonely and scared. I create these traumatic images in my mind. And while, yes, my flashbacks are based in some sort of reality, none of them are facts, none of them are real.

My mind won't shut them off. Flash. Flash. Flash. They pop into my head, so vivid and so real, yet they're not. Flash. Flash. Flash.

FORTY-SEVEN.

There's a new song on the radio I just know you'd love. It's rare for me to dip out of my genre of country music into the realm of hip hop, but every once in a while I find a song with a good beat that I can vibe to. The song came on the radio and you jumped right to my mind. I wanted to call you or send you a screenshot of my Spotify and say, "New jammmmm!" Knowing that it would instantly be one of our songs.

Those were the best times. The times when there was music and dancing. I can see your face. You'd do that little side grin thing and purse your lips together while nodding your head and shoulders to the beat. Moving your arms and hands from side to side with that cool-guy look in your eye. I'd just laugh. I miss your crazy dance moves and your break dance backflips. I miss when we would just bounce to the rhythm without a care, knowing that we could dance freely without judgment.

A good beat will always be our song. I hear you in the music and I'll save us a playlist for our next dance party, little brother.

FORTY-EIGHT.

I handed some man your car keys yesterday. Signed the title. Walked inside with an envelope of cash. Then I exhaled. It was harder than I thought. It sounds trivial, I know, but selling your car felt like selling yet another piece of you. How is it that fifteen months later it still hurts this much.

I think about what that car meant to you. How it was a status symbol you hid behind, trying to mask your pain with success. Flashy things and fancy cars. You put on a face, trying to prove to the world you were OK, but you were dying inside. I wonder if you knew that all the bling was really useless and empty; Or did you believe your own lie, as it poured out of you like truth being told through your veneers.

I gave some man your keys. Your keys. I made sure to drive it one last time, as I took my son to his first gymnastics class. I made sure to keep it on your station, nothing but hip hop all morning long. I was mindful as I felt the steering wheel and smelled the leather one last time. One more piece of you is gone.

FORTY-NINE.

I moved here for you. I didn't realize I was doing it at the time, but when a job opportunity presented itself in Las Vegas I just tossed my name in the hat, thinking nothing of it. I reflect on it now and realize I wanted to be closer to you. I knew something was wrong, I just didn't know to what extent.

Las Vegas, this desert town of neon lights and late nights. City of Sin. Never had I ever imagined my life would bring me here. I love the ocean. I love to walk barefoot in the sand. I love to ride my beach cruiser and watch the waves. But the desert was calling, for better or worse, and I'd cross the world for you, Code. I'd do it again 1000 times.

I've since made a home in the desert, even though I thought I'd never stay this long. The Strip is my back-yard. I've met a wonderful man who loves me back, and together we've created a safe home for our new son. The domino effect continues to impress me, going down the rabbit hole of "If I hadn't done this, I wouldn't have done that"—knowing that it all led me to the happiness and joy I have now.

Thank you. Thank you for bringing me here. Thank you for calling me to the desert. Thank you for trying as hard as you did, and fighting with every ounce of you, to the very last slip up. Thank you for being a guiding force for me, then, now, and always. Thank you for all that you were and are and will forever be. God, I Fucking miss you.

FIFTY.

I turned the house upside down today looking for something. I didn't find it, though I'm sure it's somewhere in plain sight. I found one of your ties though. I've gone through your boxes several times over these months. A little bit here, a little bit there. All I can ever stand is a little bit.

I remember coming across this tie and thought to myself. "Ah! This one! I'm keeping this one." I plan to save it for Austin one day, so he can have a piece of you. A tangible piece anyway.

The tie makes me smile. It's royal purple with a light blue and pink pattern. I remember you wearing it a few times. You always had to "pop" with your ties and socks. Bright colors and fancy designs. My very own fashion expert, always helping me with my own lack of style.

The tie smells like you. How do your things smell like you still? I stuck my nose into the tie, wound up in a box. Your scent lingers and for a blink it makes me feel closer to you. Our sense of smell is the only sense that isn't filtered before it hits the brain, it has a direct pathway. Our sense of smell is the strongest trigger for memories. It's science. The scent is picked up by the olfactory bulb and it runs directly to the amygdala and hippocampus. A nonstop flight right to the heart of emotional memory.

I love this tie. I love this scent. I dread the day my nose can no longer detect you in all things left behind.

FIFTY-ONE.

I looked in the mirror the other day and I barely recognized myself. I took a long stare because it didn't even look like me. The reflection felt strange, disconnected. There are dark new-parent circles under my eyes, and my eyes are tired.

I know this is what's to be expected one year into parenting, but I sensed it was more than that. In fact, I know it is. There's a glaze over my eyes, a sadness buried deep at times. Other times it's right there on the surface, and tears flow easily in the blink of a memory.

I think about the fragility of our realities. In an instant they can change and shift. I looked at my face and really observed it. So much has changed so quickly and so slowly. This is my new reality. I fear the sadness behind my eyes will last forever. Knowing this could never be true, but fearing it anyway. I vow to find the sparkle again.

FIFTY-TWO.

You know me, I'm not into movies, not like you were. But documentaries are my thing. Well, documentaries and cheesy teen romances. I've been watching a lot of documentaries lately, and a few have struck my heart.

First there was the true story of Avicii. He completed suicide less than three weeks after you died. His music brings me back to so many great nights on the dance floor. He speaks about how his anxiety became overwhelming. How the fame, women, and money didn't measure up. He states, on film, that he just couldn't take it anymore.

Then the documentary about the young man in Massachusetts who was coaxed into suicide by his girlfriend. "I love you, now die." A documentary with footage of a young boy, speaking into the camera just days before his death, confessing that his social anxiety was unbearable, that he felt alone and too different to go on.

I'm convinced that your death was accidental. That is how it's been reported and documented and in the truth of my heart I know that you didn't mean to take Fentanyl. It's an epidemic, and a poison. However, I still see you in those films. In those young, attractive men, lost and confused, overwhelmed by the world.

Your death was accidental but the same pain lived within you. A deep, deep pain that felt so unique to you. A pain you never could bear to fully share or express with me, or anyone. I would have listened though, had you tried.

I see it all too often. That pain, that ache beyond words that leads to darkness, that leads to intolerable loneliness, tossed with shame and a side of fear. I see it in my patients, I see it splashed all over the news and in these documentaries, I see it as an increasingly common pain, which makes it falsely unique if it's everywhere.

If only we could wear our emotions on our shirts, or signs that bore our souls. If only we didn't live behind filters and Botox and appearances. If only we showed our hearts to each other, truly, there'd be no room for loneliness. We could realize that we are all in it together, we are all in this humanness. Pain and joy and fear and love. We're all in it, and we're in it all.

FIFTY-THREE.

There's a photo in our downstairs bathroom. It's of Kris and me. I'm noticeably pregnant, probably about halfway through if I remember correctly. It looks like we are on some tropical island with the water and the palm trees, but in fact we were at Lake Las Vegas. Late-March 2018. I love the photo and I blew it up, found a nice wooden frame, and hung it in the bathroom.

I don't use that bathroom often, but yesterday I did. I looked at the photo as I washed my hands with some organic lavender soap. It was then I had an ah-ha moment. I realized that photo was taken the night that you died. Well, the night before you died in the wee hours of the next morning. That's where I was, happy and pregnant, on a lake and completely oblivious to what was about to happen in my life.

A part of me wants to replace the photo. A part of me feels guilty, as if I should have magically known somehow. Should have done something, miles away. Spiraling down the rabbit hole of "if only." But another part of me feels like the photo sheds some light and perspective.

A perspective that in this exact moment, people are dying, people are giving birth, people are laughing. In this exact moment, I may be laying in my hammock in my backyard writing on my phone, and someone else's life is changing dramatically. Or someone's life is about to.

A perspective that makes the difficult moment seem small in comparison to what's out there. And the beautiful moments mean so much, because they, too, are fleeting.

I think I'll keep the photo in its wooden frame.

FIFTY-FOUR.

I'm writing to you from Canada. Our home and native land, as it's sung. One of your best friends came over today. We took Austin to the park and spoke about you while he splashed and played, waddling around in true 1-year-old fashion.

It's funny how grief is such a shared, unspeakable experience that can bring people together. He has made a point to drive an hour each way to visit me every time I'm home. I think I've seen him more in the past year than I have in the many years before, combined. And I'm so glad. He gets it. He gets this loss. He gets me when I speak about the little things. There's no explanation needed. We both knew your quirks and loved you for them. So instead of explaining to someone your mannerisms and how I miss them so much, he misses those exact mannerisms too. In all its tragedy and beauty, we are in this together.

There's something special about being around those who love you as much as I do. An energy, felt without words, almost as if your presence is magnified. I am so thankful for the friends you left behind, and how they can hold me up. How we hold each other up. Grief is funny like that.

FIFTY-FIVE.

Someone asked me the other day why I haven't written much lately. They posed a very good question with it, "Are you scared to get to 100 posts?" It was thoughtful; I sat with it for a moment, and immediately knew the answer was no.

Starting this writing journey has been immensely heal-ing, connecting, and empowering. I feel you listening somehow. Some days I have a lot to say, other days the thought of sitting with it all is just too much, so I take my rest and my self-care. 100 is just an arbitrary number that I chose. It's a nice round number. Not too small, not too grand. Just a number.

Just because I'll reach my hundredth post one day, doesn't mean I'll stop having things to say. It doesn't mean I'll feel any more or less complete than when I began. It doesn't mean that I won't ache with deep pains at times when you come into my mind. Nor does it mean that my heart will be healed and I'll live peacefully without you. I miss you all the time, in daily reminders, in all of the small ways and big ways. I don't think this will ever go away. Somehow though, life shifts, and is still shifting, and the loss of your physical presence is normalizing, for better or for worse. My heart is resilient, though bits of it are still broken.

FIFTY-SIX.

Acceptance. This topic came up today in the men's sexual trauma group therapy I led this morning. I sat with a group of men, of all ages and races, and witnessed as they spoke about finding ways to accept very shameful traumas as the only way to move forward, to move through. I sat with tears in my eyes, inspired by their words and insights. Proud of their emotional accomplishments under my watch.

Acceptance. I listened to them and thought of you, as I do. I stare at these men and think of how they used to be little boys, small and vulnerable. I see those little boys in there, behind their eyes, behind their muscles and tall frames. I see their pain, their fear. I think of you, as a little boy. I remember us then. The world was our Adventureland. The world wasn't supposed to hurt us and harm us, but it did. How does one come to accept the traumas and the secrets. As I witness these men grapple with this question, I think of you, wishing you would have found a group like this.

Acceptance. I turn to my own internal battles. Am I to accept a world without you? Do I even have a choice. I think often about my life story, who I am, how I define myself. I am my profession, I am my passions. I am my relationships and my roles in life. I am Cody's big sister, but what does that mean without you by my side? How do I talk about the brother that I had, have. How do I integrate this part into the story.

I guess I'm still working that part out...

FIFTY-SEVEN.

I dreamt of you last night. It was one of those dreams that mimicked reality, so vivid, so real. I remember parts of it clearly and the emotions have been lingering with me all morning.

We were together, our younger selves running around and playing. I was chasing you, running upstairs, and laughing. I saw your face so clearly in my mind. The swoop of blonde hair and round cheeks. When I look at my son, I see you. I remember us then.

In the final flutters before waking, in the Theta state of dreams, just on the precipice of opening my eyes, I had a thought. What a nice dream I thought, what a fun memory, I want to tell Cody about it as soon as I wake up. And all within the same split second my heart sank, still in a dreamlike state, and the realization that you are gone came flooding in. I felt a shift in my energy, a small panic, almost as if I was hearing it for the first time over again.

I moved my body, shifting in my bed, tossing and turning to wake. Opening my eyes, I felt the sadness linger from my dream, into my day. The pit that sits in my stomach, curbing my appetite.

I exhale, and press on into the morning, wishing to return to what was. Wishing it just wasn't so.

FIFTY-EIGHT.

My son is teething, four teeth at once, and he's been up screeching in pain on and off for over an hour past his bedtime. It's been an extra-long day, I've barely stuffed a previously frozen burrito into my mouth, and I drop everything to rock him and hold him. I let him lay on my chest until he falls asleep.

I've so much to do, but letting his little hand wrap around me as he listens to my heartbeat, that's the only place I know I need to be. My body is his home. I'm his safe place. I think about those moments in life, when all you need is your mom. It's hard for me to remember what it felt like, to be scooped up into our mama's arms, knowing everything was alright. It feels like so long ago.

That's what was missing for you. You never felt safe, the way Austin does on my chest. I get it, I struggle with feeling safe too. It's that panicky feeling, a sense of being unsettled, even when you're completely fine. You didn't know how to find that feeling, not since she died. I know it well, I was right there too. You felt lost and small, looking for anything to give you that sense of being whole, even if it was a substance-induced lie.

I've heard patients describe heroin as a warm blanket, a euphoria unlike any other. I'll never know from experience, but that sure does sound like something nice to go home to, especially if you were only 11 when your safe place was taken from your little hands.

My heart breaks over these thoughts. I understand our mother now through empathic eyes. I think about what it was like for her, holding her perfect little boy, letting him lay on her chest all night, as he cried from sore gums, even though she was stripped of energy. You, the perfect little boy.

I think about her own heartache, knowing she had to leave us, knowing she was taking our first home. These thoughts make me cry. So I hold Austin tightly, and whisper to him that I love him, hoping that my words echo across time and space, praying that he always feels safe. Praying that he never feels lost. Wishing somehow you could have heard our mother's echoes, if only that could have kept you alive.

FIFTY-NINE.

It's overdose awareness day. It only gets a day? Just one day? Even breastfeeding gets a whole month. And don't get me wrong, I am a full supporter of breastfeeding. It was one of the most magical things I have done as a mother thus far. Nonetheless, its importance somehow doesn't amount to the awareness and attention that overdose needs, deserves, demands.

Every day of my life is overdose awareness day. Every. Fucking. Day.

Every day I am blatantly aware that you're not sitting next to me, laughing with me as I watch Austin play his own version of hide and seek, where he hides in plain sight, giggling hysterically. When I'm home visiting our family, there's a painful awareness that you're gone, and we are left with a lingering emptiness.

Every day is overdose awareness day for me, for our family, for thousands and thousands of other families, who lose children and siblings and parents and partners to this corrupt addiction that is so sorely misunderstood and so dismissed, until it happens to you. Until it's your brother who you're mourning.

I am thankful that there is a day where we wear purple ribbons and spread awareness on a large scale. I am thankful for the platform to speak up, to grieve out loud. But this world is in desperate need of change, and one day just isn't going to cut it.

SIXTY.

Why? Why? WHY. Whyyyy. Why me? Why you! Why? Why Please. Just tell me, FUCKING WHY. I plead and plead and plead, knowing it changes nothing.

Bargaining

"You don't want reality to be the way it is."

I immediately sobbed. It was one of those perfect moments in therapy where you just feel so completely understood. I shook my head as it hung low, tears rolling down my cheeks and dripping onto my thighs. He was right—Yossi Shahar, my therapist, an amazing and intuitive healer. He was spot on. Even years later, some days I simply cannot stand that this is my new reality. I refuse to. I feel like a child, arms crossed, pouting and stomping. *No. This can't be real. I will not accept it. No. No. No.*

I think that is the best way to describe the bargaining phase of grief. It's when you do not want life to be what it is. It's similar to denial, which is more of a shocked state. You're in denial because it's too much to process. That slowly thaws, and you begin to comprehend the new reality. *He's gone. He is dead. I will never hug him again.* You start to think about what this new reality, without them, means. And even though the shock has worn off, your brain just cannot accept this new truth. Remember when I said that your brain loves you? It truly does. Your brain is so caring; it will get wildly creative to come up with some "life deals" that you'll beseech the world to make with you. This is bargaining.

It's going back and spiraling down the rabbit hole of what ifs. It's the phase where you become obsessed with playing detective. Asking thousands of questions, just doing anything and everything to find where it all went wrong; to find a glitch in the matrix or to prove that it's all a bad dream. *This can't be true. This can't be real.* You will play the story in your head, filling in the blanks where you don't know the answer, making up a new ending. When I was a kid I loved the "choose your own adventure" books; you got to turn left or right, and it would take you to a different ending, with the same characters. This is what bargaining is like. You know you can't actually change anything, but you spend countless hours laying in your bed, staring at the ceiling, choosing different directions throughout the story.

If he had gone to a different rehab center, this wouldn't have happened. If he hadn't lived in Las Vegas, the city of sin, for so many years, he would have never turned to substance use like this. If he had never broken up with that girlfriend, the really nice one, maybe things would have been different. The points in the story that your mind goes to range from minutes before their death to years back. From small, seemingly insignificant details to all of life's big-decision moments. I know that after Cody died, I put on my detective hat for months. I reached out to his friends and ex-girlfriends. I stalked his social media, looking for "clues" or something that could pinpoint the moment when it all went wrong. I replayed the story of his life, like a film in my head, as I lay awake at night. Diving into the memories, dissecting every conversation in my head. Using my hindsight bias to show me what was suddenly so clear. Convincing myself that *this, this was the moment* and if I could just go back in time, I would warn him, stop him, protect him, lock him up and never let him leave my sight.

Personally, now, I feel torn in my mental search back through time. I think about if a genie in a magic bottle appeared to me and asked me, "Would you like to go back in time and save your brother?"

First of all, I am not sure I would know where to go. My instinct tells me to go back to our childhood, to find a better way for us both to cope with the grief of losing our mother. To find a way to set us up with a better foundation to deal with adulthood. Or perhaps I'd go back even further, to tell my mother to go to the doctor earlier. If they found the tumor sooner, would she have had a chance? If I could go back in time, which memory would I jump to? I spend never-ending nights thinking about this.

Let's say I decided; I came to an agreement with myself on which memory I would go back to. So now I tell the genie, "Yes, please send me back to this day, at this time, and let me change the path of my life, and of Cody's life." The magic genie, a creation of my wild imagination, says to me, "OK, on the count of three, I will snap my fingers, and poof, you'll be there, ready to save the day." It's at that point in my imagination that I hesitate. I pause. The mental bargaining continues. *If I go back in time and change everything, what else will change?* This is where I stop. "Can I still end up with my husband and son? Can my dad still find Julie, my current stepmom, whom I love and adore? Can I still grow into the woman I am today, even without every piece of the puzzle that made me? What would the consequences of going back in time be? Knowing what I know about the butterfly effect, I realize that if I changed one thing, my entire life could be different. Would I do it? Would I do it if it meant saving Cody? What bargain am I willing to make with this genie who actually doesn't exist?

This mental play, this is bargaining. This is what the mind does. It creates magic genies and other methods of time travel. It pleads with the Universe at large and that big man above. *Please, God, if I am good, if I promise to be kind and selfless, can you some way, somehow, just bring him back?* When you're in the state of bargaining, you will beg with desperation from your core, giving absolutely anything to change your new reality. *Whatever it takes, anything, please, just...please.*

....
....

When Cody died, I had so many unanswered questions. So many pieces that didn't make sense. My mind did what any mind would do, it filled in the blanks. I created a story with as much as information as I could. This was the detective phase; I think it's pretty common after an unexpected death, especially when there are so many secrets involved. The world of addiction and substance use is chock-full of secrets and darkness.

Did it hurt? Where was he? Where was he going? Why was he alone? Where did he buy drugs? Where did he use? What did he think he was buying? Was this on purpose? Was this an accident? Could he have known it was Fentanyl? Was this a poisoning? What was going through his head? Was he in pain? Did he know how much I loved him? Did he give up? Why wasn't someone there? Where were the facility supervisors? Why didn't someone say anything? Why the fuck was he alone?

Months after his death, I was introduced to an extraordinary podcast called *Last Day*. Jessica Kordova Kramer and Stephanie Whittles Wachs both lost their brothers to the opioid crisis, so they got together and created *Last Day*, among many other wonderful podcasts. When Jessica randomly found my Instagram and messaged me to listen, it absolutely changed my life. Every week I would wait for a new episode, and my commute became not only more enjoyable that day, but therapeutic. Every episode is brilliant, but one of them that particularly moved me was episode four. The episode is titled: "Was It Painful?" When I listened to that episode, it was like they were broadcasting my personal thoughts. They were describing everything that I, too, felt. They spoke about their questions and the manic detective phase of bargaining. They got me...and I felt just a little less alone. Because of this podcast, I can assure this phase is universal.

I had questions. My mind spun with questions. I did some digging, finding out new truths. Sometimes these truths were painful. Sometimes I wished I hadn't dug so far into Cody's past. This is when I realized some of these questions might best be left unanswered. It was sobering, to think that maybe it was best to close my newfound detective agency and retire Cody's memories as is. It took, and still takes, a lot of self-restraint, but I believe this is the best case for me.

Do I really need to know who introduced him to heroin for the first time? Do I really need to know about the moments in his life that he was most ashamed of? Those moments and that shame, that's what fueled his addiction. It was a dark, perpetual cycle. Pain led to using, which led to shame and more pain, which led to more using. And on and on and on. I realized that I do not need to search down a history that would only hurt me to know. His dark past is what took him from me, and that has already hurt me enough.

I came to these realizations and stopped my hunt, what I was looking for was surely no pot of gold at the end of a rainbow, and it would never bring him back. I gave myself a reality-check. I spent many moments in my car, on a walk, or during a yoga class just talking myself through this rationalization. *You don't need to know that, Nicole. What will knowing that do for you? What if you find out an answer that you don't like, one that is painful? Why are you torturing yourself? Let it go.*

....

....

I was on the phone with one of my best friends, describing my writing and this book. I told her that I was authoring five chapters to go along with the hundred love letters. Compiling them as an autobiographic memoir as opposed to a self-help guide. Much like the *Last Day* podcast was my therapy, I truly hope that my words, which convey my grief experience, can serve as therapy to someone. She asked me, compassionately, "What stage of grief do you think you're in now?"

I paused to give it some thought. "I guess it changes," I replied, still looking inward for the answer. "I think I've reached acceptance, but I don't know that I'm always there. There are days when I feel like I've accepted this, but perhaps it's just that I'm used to it now. Some days I feel angry and rageful. Some days I feel very sad. I think I'm in acceptance more often than not though." I paused, continuing to think out loud and spill my heart in a nonlinear fashion, knowing she was without an ounce of judgment. "Actually, to be honest, I struggle with bargaining a lot still. I spend a lot of time in my mind going back to memories and playing out the scenarios. I think about what I wish I would have done. I make up a story that if I just did this or that, he wouldn't be gone. Even though I find waves of acceptance, I think I drift into the bargaining phase pretty frequently." She listened and allowed me to process, as best friends do.

When I talk about this, it feels like ten different memories flash through my mind at once. *That is when I should have done something different. That moment. No, that one. Or maybe that one.* Admittedly, from time to time, I find it very hard to believe I couldn't have saved him. I have this fantasy that *if only I knew what I know now*, everything could have been different. It's a painful thought, but like a dull pain that just aches in the background. I am not exactly sure if these thoughts will ever go away. I am not sure I want them to either. At times, I enjoy escaping into my mind, playing out a scene, and changing the ending. Closing my eyes, and even if for just a brief imaginary moment, creating a world where Cody still exists by my side.

I suppose the only "cure" for the bargaining thoughts is acceptance.

SIXTY-ONE.

I'm in California this weekend, a state that feels like home. I'm out here for my dear friends' wedding. The venue was gorgeous, the company was buckets of fun. It was the type of wedding where every guest is on the dance floor until the very last song. We all kicked our heels off and, with wild bare feet, jumped around for hours.

There was a moment, in all of the shaking and twirling, that I paused internally. I stopped for a moment, and took it all in. It was a state of true mindfulness. I was on the dance floor, moving and grooving, but I was also the observer, witnessing the joy, the love, and the fun, right in front of me.

It's moments like this that get me. I have to pause and take a breath. I thought to myself, "There truly is happiness in this life. And this moment, right here, right now...

this is happiness." I looked around at all of my friends, smiling and dancing. This is a good, good moment.

I love moments like this, even though they automatically turn bittersweet. Were you not able to see the joy in this world? Were you unable to feel this type of love and connection? Where did we fail you? Did you forget that you too were invited onto the dance floor?

SIXTY-TWO.

Tonight, the air was still. It was one of those nights with absolutely no wind. I sat in my backyard, staring up at the palm trees, just waiting for a breeze, for a gentle rustling. Nothing. The stillness was piercing. I thought of you, and decided to re-watch the video we played at your funeral.... at your celebration of life. Some celebration.

Then, with tears, I re-read my eulogy. It was like I needed to feel you again, to feel connected to the emotions. Like pressing a bruise just to see if it still hurts.

It still hurts.

Maybe it always will?

SIXTY-THREE.

I'm starting to get more into advocacy. For a while, I couldn't even tolerate sitting in a room where the words "drugs" or "overdose" or "substances" were even spoken. It was all too triggering, all too much. I didn't want to advocate for the cause of ending the opiate crisis because I didn't give a fuck. I didn't want to help anyone else, nor save a life, because it wouldn't bring you back. So why bother? Why should I.

But that was my pain talking. I've started speaking up and speaking out. I've become open minded to participating in overdose awareness events and even recently agreed to partner with some friends at a non-profit here in Las Vegas to educate on overdose and Naloxone. These are big steps for me. And as I take them in stride, I know you are proud. I feel that I am not doing this work for me, but for you.

This is your mission, and I plan to fulfill it. This is our mission. Even when you were deep in the trenches of your own addiction, you always spoke about helping others on a grand scale. In your day to day, you were the most kind, loving, and helpful soul. Always giving the shirt off your back. No one would deny that. And you wanted to do more.

I remember our last phone call. We spoke over Face-Time. I treasure that call. It was just 36-hours before your final breath. You told me about your goals to move into sober living, to give back, to mentor others, to fight for yourself, and to help others in their fight.

This is now our fight. I'll stand front and center for you. Always have, always will.

SIXTY-FOUR.

Last night, I went into my son's room before I went to bed. He's had the flu this week and I wanted to make sure his temperature had broken. It had. But the digital forehead thermometer woke him from his sleep. He cried and I tried to sneak out, but he kept crying, so I placed my hand on his back. I rubbed his back for a while, and every time I took my hand off, he would whimper. I tired of standing so I decided to crawl into his crib and lay with him.

I'm much too tall for this tiny crib, but I crunched myself into a little ball to comfort my sweet boy. This is love.

I thought of you.

I thought of that night, a few short years ago, it was a Thursday, and I had just gotten home from a sound bath. My cell rang, and you were on the other side. "Nix, I need help," you said, shaky. "Where are you? What's going on?"

I pleaded for answers. The call dropped, and my heart sank. It was 10pm, I was in pajamas, ready for bed, but I had to find you. I panicked.

My phone rang again. I answered. You had phoned me from your hotel room. Your phone had died. "What hotel are you at? I'm coming."

I jumped into my car and drove an hour to the border, where California and Nevada meet. I parked the car and raced inside. Marching up to the second floor, I knocked on your door. I had a million questions. *Why were you there? Alone. What were you doing. Why weren't you home, safe. What's going on?*

But when you opened the door, I saw your face, and I hugged you. We didn't speak. I looked at the king-sized bed and crawled onto it. "Come here," I said, motioning my arms to you. And you did; 6 foot 2, muscles and all. You sighed, relieved to see me and my love. We sat there for 30 minutes in silence and tears. I held you. I told you I loved you. I gave you one of my famous pep-talks about how it was all going to be OK. That we always, always have each other. I held you.

I took you back home with me that night. Made up the guest-room and tucked you in. I wish I never let you leave the next day. I wish I had asked more questions. I wish I was still holding you.

Last night, scrunched in that crib, I realized, "This is all we need." We all just need to be held.

SIXTY-FIVE.

I listened to Trevor Noah's book on Audible. It was excellent, and I love that it's narrated by him. He writes about his life, growing up poor in South Africa during and just after the end of apartheid. I was listening to him talk about his mom and her discipline, he said, "Sometimes you give your children tough love, when all they really need is love."

This. This statement hit me and shook me and rang so very true for me. This reminder of something I learned the hard way. This sentence will impact the way I parent my children, and the way I treat others for the rest of my life.

With addiction, it is said, that there is a fine line between enabling and love. It is encouraged even, in the psychology literature, to set firm boundaries and to use tough love when dealing with someone in your family who struggles with substance use. And while I don't entirely disagree, I think this is very, very tricky.

I remember, Oct 2016, when you were at the worst I'd ever seen you. I'd just been informed that you left your 3rd rehab facility much before the 6-week program was over and we weren't sure exactly where you were. You had threatened to leave, and when I spoke to you, I felt you were being irrational, closed-off, aggressive, and I couldn't for the life of me understand why you were so unwilling to stay, to work the program. I even took it personally. As if you didn't love our family, or me, enough to stay in treatment.

I was exhausted, desperate, scared for your life, and feeling unstable in my own. I made a very, painfully difficult decision. I decided to cut you off. I'd never so much as not answered a call or text from you within minutes of receiving it. And here I was, deciding to cut our connection. At the time, I convinced myself it was self-care for me, and tough love for you.

I regret but a few things in life, and this ranks high on my list; it might even be at the top. We didn't speak for four months. I blocked your number and refused to answer unknown calls.

Cody, if I could take those four months back, I would. I'd answer every call, and find a way to be there for you, in your pain and in your suffering. I now see that "tough love" wasn't what you needed. You just needed love. You were confronting demons and they scared you shitless. You wanted to run, so you ran.

If I could do it all again, I would have seen that this was exactly when you needed me closer, not further. My love should never come with conditions. I am forever sorry.

SIXTY-SIX.

I was talking to Julie a few days ago. I've always said, she's sent from above. I truly mean it. I believe Mom had a conversation with the Universe and a hand in bringing her into our lives. She's a blessing of a stepmom; the reason our broken family feels whole. She glues us together. I always think, if only, if only, her love could have come sooner... where would you be now.

We were talking about blame, guilt, and shame. Namely, the self-blame we both feel for letting you down, somehow convinced we could have changed the story "If we knew then what we know now." But, this isn't one of those choose your own ending story-books. That's not how it works, much to my dismay.

She told me to be kind to myself. She reminded me that the guilt and blame I hold is unfounded and damaging to my healing. She's right. Despite the millions of moments

I look back on and convince myself I could have saved you, I know for some reason it was meant to be this way. The old cliché. "But why didn't he tell us how bad it really was? Why didn't I know?" "Shame," she said. Shame.

You held such crippling shame. Such crippling, damaging, secret shame that you hid from us all, behind a crooked smile and bright green eyes. "This is why we must change the conversation, change the culture." She reminded me of our mission.

Our culture views substance use disorders as disgusting, beneath us, wrong, and ugly. The language surrounding addiction is harmful, dehumanizing, and shaming. Don't get me wrong, I'm not promoting the idea that we beautify addiction. I'm promoting the idea that we humanize it. That we normalize the human desire to run from pain and escape suffering. That we empathize with those who choose to numb and spiral down the rabbit hole.

I'm asking the world to see you first. To see Cody Anders as a brave and loving young man, who took a wrong turn and didn't know how to find his way out. I'm asking the world not to judge you without knowing your story. I'm asking the world to realize that your struggles were the least interesting thing about you, and to remember that you were so much more than a man who died from an accidental overdose. You had nothing to be ashamed of, if only you knew.

SIXTY-SEVEN.

The temperatures have dropped in Las Vegas. A crisp, fresh 65 degrees this morning and I love it. I put on a sweater, grabbed a pumpkin latte, and started listening to Christmas music. A little preemptive, I know. I can hear you chuckle. But you know me and the holidays, my favorite time of year. I love the lights and the music and magic. I love that people tune into their kindness, even though it's been there year-round. I love that the weather calls for cocooning and cuddling. I look forward to October, November, and December all year.

Just like with any changes in season, memories stir up, and I find myself missing you. It will be our second winter without you. A little less painful perhaps; there's nothing like the sting of the first.

Remember when I first moved to Vegas and we moved in together. Well, I moved into your house. The one you purchased when you were just 22. Who owns a house at 22? The world was at your fingertips, if only you knew.

It was mid-September, and the weather was turning, just as it is now. We spent every day together for those wonderful winter months. We put up Christmas lights and I made you go tree shopping with me. We had Fall and Winter scented candles and warm lattes. It truly is the most wonderful time of the year.

And yes, while it's a bit early to let my heart flutter with the idea that the holidays are around the corner, I know if you were here you would just be along for the ride. Laughing at my childlike joy. I'm missing you the most right now.

SIXTY-EIGHT.

I met with a friend yesterday who owns a publishing company and we talked about turning these love letters to you into a book. That's what they are, love letters, even the ones where I'm angry, hurt, or confused. All of my words are completely fueled by love.

The funny thing is, I was hesitant to share my posts publicly at first, and now I'm considering binding them and distributing them to the world.

First of all, it's terrifying. When you put yourself and your opinions out there, there are bound to be judgments and criticisms. Luckily, I think my skin is growing thicker with age. I can hear you say, "Let the haters hate." You were always my biggest cheerleader, in all of my goals and pursuits. I tried to be yours too.

Secondly, I fear judgment not of me, but of you. Of your story. Or your life, and most importantly, of your death.

I fear the slandering of your name and others replacing it with words like Junkie or Addict. I fear that exposing your story would be harmful in some way.

But then, I sit back, and I realize that sharing all sides of this story is exactly what the world needs in order to shift perspectives and change conversations. The world needs to know who you really were. And what the struggle was truly about. Sharing the humanness behind addiction; this is the story I think you'd want me to tell. This is the shame-buster that we all so desperately need.

So, I'll move forward to whatever the next step is. I'll keep sharing our story and writing my love letters for the world to see.

Let the haters hate.

SIXTY-NINE.

Sometimes my mind plays tricks on me. Like just last night, in the backyard before sunset, I thought of you. You felt so distant though, like a pixelated memory of a faraway place. You were my little brother, confidant, and best friend for almost 28 years. But somehow, after just 18 months without you, this is my new normal. Somehow my mind has found a way to shift, maybe to escape the pain of your loss. This new normal, it's settling in.

Does that make sense, even a little bit? For me it's still jumbled.

I found myself thinking, did you ever really exist? I find myself asking, was this all a dream? Are the childhood memories of me with a little brother, two peas in a play-ful pod, are they even real? Or is my mind creating this strange illusion. Did Cody Anders, did he really live here, on this Earth, at the same time as me? In my same home.

Of course you did. But why do these thoughts come up? Am I the only one with such a strange pattern of thinking. Am I totally losing it, consumed by grief? Where do these ideas even come from.

It's funny how quickly we can adapt. I suppose that's the driving force of our species. For 30 years I was child-less, single, and free. Yet, now, just over a year later, I can barely remember what life was like without Austin. In the same way, for 330 months I was Cody's big sister. We were Nicole & Cody through and through. And now, sometimes, I find it hard to remember that those moments were real. I find myself writing you out of my automated answer when people ask who I am.

I don't know if this makes any sense, but for me, this mind-fuck is very real. I'm slowly accepting the idea that you're not here. And as the pain fades, you do too, yet somehow, it's twisted... that pains me more.

SEVENTY.

I listened to *The Addicted Mind* podcast during my lunch break, while I tackled 100 floors on the StairMaster. Thirty minutes never flew by so quickly; I was so engaged in the episode, as Jacob Jones shared his story. In fact, despite the public setting, I became tearful as I listened to his insights.

Jacob told his story of addiction and as I listened, it was like I was listening to you. He was answering questions I always wanted to ask, but now I don't have the chance to. He was sharing, so vulnerably, his journey through deep opiate addiction. Just like you, he started out with personal insecurities and anxieties in the world. He is from a loving family, and even played college football. He was just a "regular" young man who was prescribed a pain-killing medication. From a medical doctor. Fucking doctors.

That's where it all began, and then it spiraled. Just like you. As I listened, I heard you in every step of his story. He is three years without substance use and highly engaged in helping others. This, too, was your dream.

It simultaneously breaks my heart and brings me such joy when I hear stories like his. To know it's possible to come out of the throes of darkness and into higher purpose and community. I've always known it was possible. I never, ever, ever lost hope for you. Not until that awful phone call.

Why wasn't hope enough?

SEVENTY-ONE.

I drove to work this morning, as I do every Monday to Friday. The same route, the same time. And as I pulled in I had a flashback. I remember one morning, in late March. It was a Friday morning and I had my headphones in, talking to Dad as I drove to work.

We were in the thick of it, our family. We were constantly on the phone, planning, strategizing, and even panicking about how we were going to help you. We pulled together every single time. Every slip-up, every phone call. We hopped on planes and dropped our agendas. Looking back, I know we did everything we possibly could, even though sometimes I wish we did more.

That morning, I was frustrated. Beyond frustrated. I was to my wits' end. I was pregnant and overwhelmed, feeling as though too much was being asked of me. "It's so unfair!" I asserted, in tears. I was in panic and fear, and I was angry. I was angry that we had been going through so much, for so long. I was angry that you were struggling. I was angry that I was being asked to juggle too many things on my plate. I was angry that there wasn't a magic fix.

"Honestly Dad, sometimes I think it would be better if he just died," I snipped. I felt the remorse of my words almost instantly, but a part of me meant it. I was exaggerating and using this speech to express my frustration. But a part of me meant it.

Now that you're gone, we don't call each other in panic nearly as often. We don't have family meetings to plan or strategize how to best support your sobriety. We don't have to "deal" with the highs and the lows of wondering where you are or if you'll show up for Christmas. But let me tell you this, it's not easier. It's not better in any fucking way. You're gone and nothing will ever be whole again; our hearts are broken, and I miss you every day.

I'm sorry for my words and for my anger, but I'm sure you know that. I beat myself up for a long time, because that Friday morning was your last Friday alive. Little did I know. I think the lesson here is to find the beauty in your frustration. I was so, so angry because I loved you so, so deeply. And that, that's a beautiful thing.

SEVENTY-TWO.

One of my closest friends sent me this Francis Weller quote. It so deeply resonates with me, as if he was speaking to my soul.

"Grief is subversive, undermining the quiet agreement to behave and be in control of our emotions. It is an act of protest that declares our refusal to live numb and small. There is something feral about grief, something essentially outside the ordained and sanctioned behaviors of our culture. Because of that, grief is necessary to the vitality of the soul. Contrary to our fears, grief is suffused with life-force... It is not a state of deadness or emotional flatness. Grief is alive, wild, untamed and cannot be domesticated. It resists the demands to remain passive and still. We move in jangled, unsettled, and riotous ways when grief takes hold of us. It is truly an emotion that rises from the soul."

SEVENTY-THREE.

You'd be 29 today. It's hard to believe this is the second time the earth has rotated around the sun and another Oct 12th is here without you. It's hard to believe.

Anniversaries are difficult. Just like birthdays and holidays and other days when there's a knowing in my bones that we should be together. And yet here we are, miles and worlds, and levels of consciousness apart.

Part of me wants to say I'll have a drink in your honor to celebrate... but drinking was part of the problem. So that doesn't seem right. Why do we have to become inebriated or buzzed to feel the joys of celebration in this culture? Why can't we dance and sing and breathe deeply with our precious lungs full of life-force.

Today I'll think of you even more than usual, which may very well be every waking moment. I'll dance for you. I'll find the music and play some more and I promise today

I'll make time to dance. I'll sing for you, whether a little jingle under my breath or loudly in the shower. I'll breathe deeply and intentionally, knowing you no longer can. I'll spend time with family and friends, claiming today a day of connection, joy, laughter, and love. And today, I'll talk about you, and reminisce about your beautiful life.

Today, on the day of your birth, I'll remember just that. That once upon a time, a beautiful baby boy was brought into this world. He was my best friend and little brother. He shook me to my core with all the big emotions for 27 years, and for this, I'll love him forever.

SEVENTY-FOUR.

I spent the weekend in New York City. Dahlia lives here now. One of your favorite cities. I know you would have jumped at the opportunity to come out here with me to visit her. It's truly a city of so much life, constantly buzzing. Personally, it's a bit too much for me, but I can see the appeal.

We spent the weekend, celebrating you, as promised. In many ways, your death has brought us closer together. We shared memories of you and found little reminders of you weaved into our weekend.

Manhattan is a booming city, with people zooming left and right. You can find every type of person, from all walks of life, all on one city block, crowded, hustling here and hustling there. The people watching is unlike any other city I've seen.

I've grown more sensitive when I people watch. I've grown more compassionate. My internal dialogue is not usually one of judgment, but one of curiosity. I notice that I find myself asking, *"Who is this person and where have they been?"* What is their story.

The Asian man who was rushing by and knocked into me, the woman yelling on her phone in Spanish while rocking a baby in her arms, the white guy looking lost at the train station. Who are these people and what brought them here. The homeless man or woman on every street corner. The young kids, laying on a blanket on the sidewalk. Where did they stumble and fall that brought them here.

Most times, I feel helpless to save the world, though my heart screams at me to try. So I tell myself, if I can learn to always speak and respond with compassion, that's a great start. Even if nothing changes but my own internal conversation. This is how we can save the world, from the bottom, up. From the inside, out. Can't we all just start here.

SEVENTY-FIVE.

I sat next to a young man on the plane last night. He was in his early 30s and he was clearly a bit drunk. He was slurring his words to the stewardess and she cut him off. I've never seen that before on a plane.

People were staring at him. I sat there with my headphones in, pretending to listen to music. They exchanged sharp words. He was rude; it was the booze talking… and she walked away. He seemed angry and then, almost like a child, he was pouting.

Some time passed and I took my headphones off. "What are you going to do in Vegas?" I asked. I expected him to say that he was going to a bachelor party, that was exactly how he was acting. Maybe he was even the groom? Just some wasted bachelor on a plane to Vegas.

He turned to me, surprised that I was speaking to him. He was kind. He showed me a ring he was wearing on his pinky finger. "This belonged to my brother," he said. He told me that he was going to visit his brother's grave for the first time. That he was killed in a motorcycle accident and was buried in Vegas. I was surprised by the answer. I shared my condolences. I told him it was brave of him to go. He admitted he was scared. I saw that. Behind the drunken stumbling of words, I saw that. "I get it. You're going to be great. I'm proud of you. Just embrace the emotions." He thanked me for listening.

Some more time passed, and we went back to what we were independently doing. "Good luck," I wished him as we deplaned. And that was that. It was a moment of simple, but possibly powerful connection. He wasn't just some drunk on a plane, he was a man with a story. A man with pain and fear.

This is the story behind addiction. This is the untold story behind every bar fight and intoxicated brawl. This is the story behind what meets the eye. And I'm so glad I could practice compassion in your honor.

SEVENTY-SIX.

The last day I saw you, it was a Monday. January fifteenth. I told you to meet us at my house that evening, so we could go to dinner. We had Italian food at a quirky Las Vegas restaurant on West Sahara Avenue. I liked your dish better than my own, so you offered me your leftovers to take "for lunch tomorrow." You paid for the meal. Generosity was your synonym.

We finished dinner and I drove you up the street, back to Oma's house where you were staying. It couldn't have been much later than eight o'clock. "I love you, Code, goodnight, see you soon, thanks for dinner." I'm sure it was something to that effect. And then we drove home. I went to work the next morning. Life continued on.

It would take eleven weeks for me to realize that our dinner at Capo's would be the last. Eighty-three days would go by until I received that dreaded phone call.

That's one thousand, nine hundred and ninety-two hours without seeing you when I could have. And now I can't. Now I can't.

SEVENTY-SEVEN.

I'm not OK. And honestly, I'm not sure I'll ever be... these were my thoughts as I showered the other night. Taking the time to just be with myself. Feeling a wave of hopelessness. I'm not OK without you, this is not how it's supposed to be. I feel a sudden shift into anger. Disappointment at the world, at the spirits of everything that control our fate.

Rationally I know that I am, in fact, OK. I look back on when we first lost you, comparing it to now. I recognize that I'm healing, I'm finding more joy, I'm not obsessing in grief as often as I once did. When I take a deeper look, I am very much OK. But there are these moments, mostly when I'm alone, that I again feel gutted and gutwrenched. The reality sinks in bit by bit, and I feel the heavy weight of losing you.

When we lost our mother, I was 14-years-old, and you were merely 12. Our worlds collapsed in more ways than one. Our safety was gone. Our sense of belonging, destroyed. It was like we were in a tornado, but we didn't know it. Our young minds, couldn't grasp it. I recognize now that I did not have the ability then to understand how massively my life had just changed. I didn't know the true gravity of being a motherless daughter, nor its domino effect on the rest of my life. My little brain, she just couldn't take it all in.

This loss, while different, is totally in my realm of comprehension. I'm fully aware of the injustice of losing you. Of the heartbreak I'll forever feel. Of the moments that will no longer have you in them when they turn into memories. My fully developed mind, is pained again and again as it realizes this life without you.

And while I know that I am OK, even when I'm not, I am heartsick with missing you.

SEVENTY-EIGHT.

If there's no one beside you, when your soul embarks
I'll follow you into the dark.

SEVENTY-NINE.

Día de los muertos. Day of the dead. The first of November. I suppose it's your day, now. A day of remembrance. A day of celebration. Ever since we attended an international boarding high school, you and I both have always had a huge fondness for Latin cultures, Spanish language, and of course, Mexican food. Some of my best memories of us, together as a family, were spent in San José del Cabo. Our second home. It only feels right for us to join in the celebrations de los muertos. De ti.

In Mexican culture, death is viewed as a natural part of the human cycle. Because it is. Mexicans view November 1st, not as a day of sadness, but as a day of celebration. A day when loved ones awaken and join in fiesta. I love this idea, as far-fetched as it may be. I often wonder how other cultures are able to handle death and grief with more grace and ease than we do, than I do.

In the Hawaiian culture, loved ones who have passed are continued to be spoken about in present tense. I think this is because they don't believe that physical death is a separation. I agree with them. I don't love you any less today than I did two years ago, when we were together, when there was breath in your lungs.

I often think about ways to keep you alive. In conversation, in memory, in celebration, in my actions and my words. I need you to still live on. To know my children, and one day my grandchildren. I need for everyone I ever meet to know about you. To know your love, through me. To know your big heart and selfless generosity. I need them to know of our inside jokes and sibling adventures.

I need them to also know of your darkness and your shame, so that we may all learn from this tragedy. I need your life to continue living, even if its form is not the same. Cody, you live on. You live on every day. This I assure you.

EIGHTY.

I found some courage today and went through a few more boxes. Sorting items, smelling clothing. Your scent lingers. Today I found a box of your keepsakes. I opened it, heart pounding. Holding back tears I gently sifted through old letters and photographs, finding it interesting what you chose to keepsake. To keep safe.

A letter from one of the loves of your life. A letter I'm sure you read over and over when the relationship ended. A letter from your old roommate, telling you how you were his brother, and encouraging you to make better choices. Some cards from Mommy, ones that she would leave in our backpacks. The cassette tape that she recorded for you before she died, titled To Cowboy. My new mission is to find a cassette player.

And then I found a Christmas card I had written you. Dec 2016. I remember this card so well and the debate

I had with myself before sending it. You had gone on a bender in Mexico City, probably the worst bender yet. You checked yourself out of rehab and off you went. This is when I couldn't take anymore, this is when I had to take space, to protect myself. We didn't speak from October 2016 to Feb 2017... except for this card.

Christmas rolled around and no one was speaking to you. I think Dad tried to reach out and you replied only with nasty messages, likely drug-induced. It was a rough, rough time. I couldn't, for the heart of me, let Christmas go by without speaking to you. So I sent you this card, with a family photo. My words were loving and kind, but also firm. I told you I missed you and I wished for you to find a way out of the darkness. If only I knew then what I know now.

If only I knew that you didn't choose any of this. If only I could have seen that more clearly. The fact that you saved this letter, well, it means more to me than words can say. Even in the worst of moments, knowing that we were your anchor and your lighthouse. Family first, family first.

Depression

There are days when I just weep for no reason at all, other than I miss Cody.

I felt depression come right away; quite truthfully, it crept in while shock and denial were still there. It's technically the fourth phase of grief, but I believe that it can hit the heart very early on. Like an arrow shot from a bow, piercing and shattering its fragile target. I also believe that depression and acceptance go hand-in-hand; when you begin to accept and understand that this person is gone, that this is your new reality, depression surfaces. It's heavy and aching and slows you down in every way. Depression is a swallowed sadness that buries you, making everything seem overwhelming and all too much.

For me, the sadness comes most often when I think about a future that will never be, about the potential that could have been. I think about the times with Cody I will never have again, the fact that he will never meet my children or live to have a family of his own. The depression comes storming in when I can't help but focus on the last time I saw him, the last conversation we had, the last time we, fill in the blank. It's about what will never be again. It's about what was going to but never will be. Depression brings all the nevers, and still I weep.

It's not uncommon to lack motivation or desire when depressed. Some people are even plagued with the thought, *Why should I continue to live if they are no longer here?* I suppose I am lucky that this thought never crossed my mind after losing Cody, though I know it would be normal if it had. What has kept me from the depths of depression has been purpose. Becoming a mother less than three months after losing Cody was the biggest blessing in disguise that this world could have gifted me. I often think about what my life would have been like without my son, Austin, being born as my fueling lifeforce.

I remember the first few nights after April 1, 2018. I could not sleep, and I could not take any medication because I was pregnant. Exhaustion would take over, and Kris would hold me until I fell asleep. I don't remember dreaming during these first nights, I would just crash into sleep, only to wake up a few hours later, screaming. *Noooooooooo! No. No. No. No.* I would wake up and yell, cry, and scream to the world, dead in the middle of night. I would wail and bellow into my pillow or onto my husband's chest, feeling my own chest fleetingly forget to breathe. During those first days, I could not answer my phone, despite the heartfelt messages of condolences and sorrow from friends and family. I refused to reply. I stared at the ceiling. I did not eat unless Kris brought me something prepared and said, "You need to feed the baby." I just laid there, in a pond of depression and pain, drowning. I just laid there weeping on and off for days.

....

....

After receiving the news about Cody, we knew we needed to fly home, but the thought of getting on a plane the next day was just too overwhelming. I needed a moment to lay there, unmoving, attempting to process even just a bit of what was happening.

On Tuesday, April 3, Kris drove me to an appointment with our midwife. We were flying to Canada the next day, to be at my family's home, sorting through the wreckage. My family lives 45 minutes away from the rehab center where Cody died. He died in the middle of the night, alone in the bathroom in his single occupancy room, in a place that was supposed to help him and keep him safe. He died at *Inspire Change Wellness Center* in Burnaby, British Columbia (BC). This location closed its doors within months of Cody's death. I sometimes wonder if the closure was connected to the tragedy, but I don't care to investigate. I know that they currently have a center in White Rock, another town in BC, also near our home. I am appalled that they refer to themselves as a "5-star addiction treatment center for men" and charge an exorbitant amount. I am simply fucking appalled.

On Tuesday, the day before flying, I went to an appointment with our midwife. We were originally planning a homebirth; I never wanted my child's first breath to be taken in a sterile hospital room. Kris had called our midwife, worried about me and how this agonizing grief would impact the pregnancy and our baby boy. She asked us to come in. She works out of her home in North Las Vegas. She is absolutely the person you want with you during pregnancy and labor. She is kind, warm, and nurturing. We walked in; I was a zombie. Normally I am gregarious and talkative, asking many questions and getting to know everyone around me. She had never seen me like this, like a shell of myself. She did a routine check-up and told me that Austin was perfectly healthy, despite the intense emotional pain I was experiencing. She gave her condolences and offered her wisdom on how to take care of myself and Austin as he continued to grow inside of me during this painful time.

I often wonder what impacts, if any, my grief could have on Austin's personality as he continues to grow up. I watch him now, a sensitive and smart little boy. He does not appear excessively anxious, but at times I wonder if he is overly attached. He is a true Mama's boy. Perhaps, too, his sensitivity is linked to the trauma bond we share. I wonder with curiosity as I watch him grow. I wonder what it must have been like for him, to literally live inside of heartbreak. He will never remember, consciously anyway, so I am not sure he will ever be able to tell me. But sometimes I pause to think about what those last few months inside my womb must have been like, growing next to lungs that struggled to breathe and a heart that struggled to beat.

When we drove home from the appointment that day, I began to scream and cry in the car. That's how it is with grief. One minute you're numb, shocked, zombie-like. The next minute you are raging and screaming. Then, you're crying and sobbing, feeling depressed and hopeless. These stages of grief can occur all within a five-minute span. Kris pulled the car over so I could catch my breath and he could hold my hand as I screamed. The screams and wails were unlike anything that ever had come out of me. They felt even foreign to me as I allowed them to take me over.

We pulled into our two-car garage and clicked the remote to shut the garage door. "I'm going to sit here for a little while," I told Kris. I needed to be alone. I needed to be with Austin. I needed more time before going back into the house where I fell to my knees in agony. I could not imagine how I would get through that afternoon's task of packing for our flight the next morning. As usual, Kris understood. He left me in the car and walked inside.

I paused my tears, trying to find a way to pull it together. I put both of my hands on my belly. The left hand on top, the right hand on the bottom, cradling and holding Austin. It was in that moment that I knew I could not let depression overpower my mind and body. I moved my left hand and then placed it over my own heart. I felt it beating. I knew that Cody's heart no longer could; at this point, he was somewhere in a morgue, waiting for an autopsy. Just waiting. But here I was, with not one but two hearts beating inside of me. This thought brought me back to tears. This time, my sobs were of gratitude, and I felt empowered. I felt the emotion of motherhood. To me, it's its own emotion. Nothing will ever describe it, and you can never understand it until you are a mother. It's some combination of protection, nurturing, determination, strength, and, of course, purpose. This is love. This is motherhood, and I had it pumping through my veins more than ever.

I placed my left hand back onto my belly, holding my baby. I spoke to him out loud in the car. "It's OK, baby. We are OK. Mommy is just really, really sad right now because Uncle Cody is gone, but I promise you that we are OK. We are safe. You are safe. Please feel my love. I will always protect you. Don't be scared of the grief and sadness that Mommy is feeling right now. You are safe, baby boy. You are safe." I began to rub my belly in a soothing motion as I continued to speak to him, tears streaming down my cheeks, eyes closed, reassuring him that nothing would ever stop me from loving and protecting him, not even this unimaginable depression and grief.

On June 24, less than three months after losing Cody, my water broke. I was only 34 weeks pregnant, much too early for our planned homebirth; much too early for birth, period. It was a scary few days in the hospital, where I sat in bed, doing nothing but trying to stay pregnant. Austin Phoenix was born, remarkably healthy given the prematurity, on June 27. He weighed 5lbs 7oz when we took him home five days later. I try not to tell myself the distorted story that it was *my* fault he was born too early. The guilt of a new mother is plenty without blaming yourself for a premature birth. Though sometimes I can't help but wonder if the depression, anxiety, grief, sadness, anger, and pain were just too much for him to live with in there.

On bad days, I blame myself. But on good days, I tell myself that Cody sent him to me early, knowing that the one thing that could keep me from the depths of depression and despair would be motherhood. Maybe Cody had a hand in it. I like this story better. I tell myself that he sent Austin Phoenix to me.

....

....

In Ancient Greek mythology and folklore, a phoenix is a long-lived bird that cyclically regenerates, or is otherwise born again. Associated with the sun, a phoenix obtains new life by arising from the ashes of its predecessor. The phoenix is a beautiful large bird that means rebirth and renewal. My little phoenix renews my heart every single day when he opens his eyes and says, "Mama, love you," with his bright blue-eyed smile. He has been my purpose, my motivation, my driving-force. I believe that loving him has single-handedly kept my depression from choking me into darkness.

EIGHTY-ONE.

There's an emotion that has been surfacing for me lately. A grief emotion. One I don't like to feel, don't like to dip into. I'm normally excellent at sitting with emotions... Not this one. This one has taken me over in the past, it's gotten me into some very difficult moments. It's a ruiner. It can ruin relationships, ruin days, and ultimately even ruin lives. Lately, I've been feeling waves of immense rage. Rage at systems, and governments, and just ignorant people in general.

The other day, I was driving to work and listening to a fantastic podcast. It's called *Last Day*. It's about the opiate crisis. It's incredibly well-produced, informative, and heartfelt. As I listened about medicated assisted treatment (MAT) for opiate recovery, I began feeling the rage bubble, from the bottom up. I teared up and had to stop myself from going down a what-if rabbit hole.

I felt pure fucking rage at the rehab center that you died in. I was enraged at their system, for letting you out of their sight, for taking you off MAT after only a few weeks. Who the fuck was in charge. Even now, I'm fueling with rage and clenching my jaw, just thinking about it. I feel rage at our lawmakers and the uninformed, ignorant culture we live in, where substance use is a crime. Just writing about this, my eyes are filling up with tears. My stomach is in angry knots.

I feel rage at myself. I'm a goddamn psychologist, but I didn't know. I didn't know enough about MAT or about what resources to use. I was grasping, making semi-educated guesses. All the while, I held the belief that MAT was "still drugs" and I wanted you off. I feel rage at all the times I insisted that this was somehow a choice. Or the time I suggested that yoga would be a magic fix, just because it helped me. How naive that statement was. I feel so much fucking rage at all of the steps in the wrong direction, made by you and me and so many others.

The knowledge is out there. Resources are out there. How many people have to die for someone important enough to give a shit and take reform seriously. It's not happening fast enough. I feel rage at all of it. I feel rage at the helplessness I felt then, and still feel now.

EIGHTY-TWO.

I threw my back out. Oh the pains of being 31. It has been absolutely killing me. The pain is on the edge of unbearable and it's been ruining my mood every day. It was to the point where I was hobbling to walk and breathing through sharp shooting pains from my back, down my legs. Easily a 9 out of 10 on the ole pain scale. Am in painting a good enough picture? You get it, the pain was very real, and very painful.

I have some hydrocodone leftover from my cesarean, when your stubborn little nephew decided he was going to stay breach. I decided that maybe it would be a good idea to take some of it. So I could try to sleep and heal the pain and not wake up every hour with a spasm. It's a painkiller, this is what it's meant for, I told myself as I sat in the bathroom, staring at the little white pill.

Knowing my low tolerance for any medication, I decided to cut it in half. Just a small, small dose. The pain wasn't letting up. I swallowed the pill and felt my mind panic. So many wild and automatic thoughts came rushing to my mind. Thinking that this is where it all began for you. Needing so desperately to numb both physical and emotional pain.

I felt more anxiety and I began to cry. I had the thought, *What have I done? What if I have a bad reaction? What if my heart stops, just like yours did.* Talking myself down from this mental ledge, challenging my cognitive distortions, reassuring myself that this was OK. I was using this medication correctly, yet cursing it for its very existence.

The pain subsided quickly and I slept through the night. The opiate worked. It helped. And dare I say it, the tiny small half of a pill of hydrocodone, it made me feel relaxed, good even. Terrified at my own thoughts, I realized…. I get it.

I mean, I don't get it. I've never struggled with addiction. Not to medication or substances, anyway. But… for a split second, I felt like I clearly understood the desperation to take away the pain, the relief that came with the pill, and even the desire the next day to feel that relief again.

I fucking get it. How frightening.

EIGHTY-THREE.

I haven't been writing you as often. Which scares me. Mostly because I notice that instead of writing, I'm numbing with my phone. It's basically 2020 and we all do it, for fuck's sake. I've been binging on social media and Netflix, it's a true addiction. Obviously one that's slightly less harmful to my health than heroin, but, only slightly.

I haven't been wanting to feel the big emotions that have been surfacing. Maybe I can blame it on the holidays or the cold weather, but I've been feeling obsessive about your death again. I've been searching through articles and listening to podcasts, incessantly, learning about the opioid crisis, about the mechanisms of addiction. I'm desperate to understand. Angry at myself for not being this invested when it counted. Mind-blown at the world and its inhumane politics and policies.

I've been extra on-edge and sensitive, knowing I'll be going home for Christmas without you. Another year without you. Not that you typically made it to family Christmas anyway. So, in some ways, not hanging your stocking won't be out of the ordinary. This pains me, so so deeply.

I haven't been writing you, but you've been swirling through my thoughts at one million miles per hour. Somehow, the longer it's been since I've seen you, the more painful and surreal this whole thing continues to get. This whole grief thing. I'm desperate not to forget you, but terrified to hold on.

The reality is, I'll grieve forever

EIGHTY-FOUR.

There's a photo of us from Thanksgiving, maybe seven years ago, at Oma's house. I remember you showed up late, with your girlfriend at the time. I was so irritated, probably made a snide comment about it. Did I make things unnecessarily difficult for you? I'm sorry. I keep saying that, I know. I'm sorry, I'm sorry, I'm sorry. I think guilt is the grief emotion that I'm just so stuck in.

I think perhaps it has to do with the way you died. With the addiction, I convince myself that you were save-able. And I feel guilt for falling short. Had you died of cancer or even a car accident, I'd probably have a different grief entirely. I obsess about my inability to save you, my inability to protect you. I'm trying to shake this part of me. How do I make it stop.

Acceptance. This stage of grief feels "the best" if you will. I look at myself and think about times when I am in acceptance of this loss. Am I in acceptance when I move through my days with ease? Am I in acceptance when I continue to live my life, enjoying moments? Am I in acceptance when I don't buy you any Christmas gifts, knowing you won't be there to open them.

Is this acceptance, or is this a big game of denial. My mind protecting me by numbing out the pain. I'm honestly not sure.

Sometimes, I think I'm in acceptance when I think about the pain that you're no longer in. When I think about the worst case scenarios of what could have been, had your addiction continued for years and years. Sometimes, I feel acceptance of some fate and plan that is mysterious and unknown, placating my emotions by believing in the magic of the universe. "It's all happening exactly as it's meant to," I whisper to myself, nudging my heart into acceptance.

Do you think I'll ever get there?

EIGHTY-FIVE.

I was speaking to one of my closest friends tonight over dinner, and then tea, about metaphysics and altered states of consciousness. Many theories speak about each person having the entire universe inside of them, how we are all connected, beyond time and space. A very interesting twist on the conversation led us to discuss shadow work. We forget about this piece, and so do most metaphysicists. We forget that, while we dance and relish in these beautiful theories and concepts of oneness, oneness also includes the dark energy, the shadow.

Too often we hear modern day hippies and spiritualists state that we are all one, chanting their namaste after yoga and speaking about the beautiful love and bright light that we all are a part of. And yes, you'd remind me, I am one of those people, too. I do think it's wonderful to feel so interconnected in love and light.

But, we must remember, that having the entire universe connected to you, also means the darkness. This means, you also have racisms and prejudice, hatred and violence, living and swirling inside. We mustn't forget that within all of us also exists the exact qualities that we despise in our worst enemies. The qualities of those we judge and shun. Metaphysics believes that the entire universe lives within us, which includes all of the ugliness in the universe, too.

This made me think of you. The true you. The whole being that is or was Cody Anders. The light and the love, the pain and the darkness. The entire universe lived inside of you and you inside of it.

It is important that we remember this. For me, losing you so tragically has taught me this lesson. The lesson of the shadow side. The beauty of the shadow side. That for every shadow, there is light.

EIGHTY-SIX.

Today, I'm wearing the necklace with your ashes inside of it. It's a tiny gold necklace in the shape of a heart. If you unscrew the top, you can peek in to see the grey ashes, almost like dust, sitting inside.

When I was first gifted this necklace, I wore it every single day. Psychologically I convinced myself it kept you closer to me. Today, I chose it mostly because it looks cute with my new beige sweater. I'm just being honest, and I think you of all people would appreciate the fashion sense.

It's not that I don't feel like this necklace is special. As I put it on this morning I thought of you and even did a double-take to be sure if I wanted to wear it, to feel you a little more present today. I find myself touching it, taking a pause and an exhale, really feeling you.

But you're not inside of this necklace. I've known that from the start. You're not in the clothes I've chosen to keep of yours, or even the photos I have framed around my house. These reminders are special and important, but I'm realizing they're just things. Special things, but things nonetheless.

Is it cliché to say that you actually live on in my heart. In my memory. In my entire being. I hold the love we share inside of my every cell, beyond the tangible necklaces and sentimental objects. Sometimes when I'm away from it all, disconnected from materialism and Wi-Fi, that's when I'm with you the most. In moments of peace, when the wind blows just so. There you are.

I love this necklace, but I feel myself moving into a new layer of grief, one where I don't have to hold on so tightly. It's comforting and freeing, all at the same time.

EIGHTY-SEVEN.

I was violently ill last week with the flu. It came on all at once and hit me out of nowhere. Within an hour, I was driving home from work early, shaking, with chills up and down my spine. My teeth were chattering when I got home and I curled up into a ball. My entire body hurt, like my nerves were all exposed, my arms and legs hurt to the touch. Head pounding as if someone was hitting it, repeatedly, with a baseball bat. I hadn't been that sick in years.

Hours into the sickness, I felt completely helpless and vulnerable. Thankfully my son was asleep and I curled up into my husband's chest and began to cry. I started to wail, big big tears. He sat and listened to me and I said, "I miss Cody. Being sick makes me think of Cody." I couldn't help but think of you, strange as that may seem.

I thought of what I've learned about being 'dope sick' and coming down from opiates. I've learned so much since you've been gone, so much I wish I knew earlier. I've learned that the withdrawal is compared to the worst case of the flu, and here I was, with my own worst case of actual influenza. Suddenly I stepped into empathy, into your world. What must it have been like. The desperation, just make it stop. Last week, in my tears, I would have given anything just to make the pain go away. The all-consuming body ache.

I fell into a fit of tears for nearly thirty minutes. I wanted so badly to feel better, but I truly wanted nothing more than to turn back the hands of time, find you in these moments of sickness, hold you, rock you, and tell you I love you. I love you.

EIGHTY-EIGHT.

Home for the holidays, without you. I definitely expected to feel these moments of sadness, this was expected. Spending time with our family brings light to your absence. When we are all together, it becomes somehow more obvious that you're not here.

Your last several years, you didn't make it to Christmas. One excuse after the next, all a part of your hiding game. But even if we were nearly certain you wouldn't show, we'd hold a spot for you at the table, and a stocking with the letter C was always on hand. Just in case. Eventually we learned not to get our hopes up... but who am I kidding, they were always up.

This year, and last, we knew with certainty that you wouldn't show. The finality of it, the permanence. It's been heartbreaking.

I like to fantasize about what toys you'd buy for Austin. How you'd spend hours chasing him around the tree, he loves playing peek-a-boo. I like to dream of you here, joining in the argument of what movie we should all watch, only to spend over an hour just browsing. In all the moments without you, I find myself imagining what you'd do or say, if only you were here.

I miss you the most on days like these. We all do.

NINETY.

Two years ago, I urged you to please come home for Christmas. Much to my pleasant surprise, you agreed. Thinking back, I don't remember the last Christmas we spent together. In 2015, we were living together, and I made you buy a tree with me. We proceeded to Target to buy white twinkle lights. I have a photo of you, on a ladder outside, with a sarcastic smile that says "I'm doing these damn lights, are you happy now?" So that was Christmas-y, even though you were nowhere to be found on the 25th.

Sitting here, my mind is recounting Christmases. Certain you weren't there in 2014, nor 2013. Perhaps we were together in 2012? I've lost count. Needless to say, your agreement to fly home for the holidays elated me. Especially because I had a secret to share. I had it perfectly planned. "Only the best brothers get promoted to uncle." I specially ordered a sticker, placed it on a Jones soda bottle (in lieu of beer, because, well, addiction). I was going to 'ice' you with this ridiculously surgery soda pop that reminds me of our childhood.

It was Dec 24th and you were set to arrive that night. A wonderful gift. I was antsy with anticipation. We set up a bed in the office because it was a full house, my favorite kind of house. Your stocking was stuffed. I remember the lavender scented lotion I put in your stocking, because self-care solves everything, right? You secretly loved lotion and all things to manscape.

And then, the phone call. My heart sank. Panic ensued. I felt your panic, it fueled mine. I began to cry. Sob. "Nix, I can't find my passport." I looked at the clock, no way you were going to make your flight. What do you mean, I insisted? You replied with a story of searching high and low, it was nowhere in sight. Looking back, I'm sure you were high. You sounded helpless to find your passport, but you were truly helpless to the addiction.

You didn't make it to Christmas. Your last Christmas on Earth.

Dad and Julie found your passport when they cleaned out your one bedroom apartment. It was right there.

Christmas has been missing you for years now, but I'll just never get used to it.

EIGHTY-NINE.

It's good to laugh at yourself. When I realized I jumped from eighty-eight to ninety, I laughed. I wasn't surprised. Between mom-brain and grief-fog, tossed up with my constant low-level state of anxiety, it's a wonder I counted correctly up to this point.

I've been trying to analyze a potential hidden meaning behind the jump. Was it a Freudian slip? Maybe I'm over-thinking it, but I came up with a correlation to the year 1989. The year between you and me. The only full year I wasn't a big sister. The year was all about me, and while normally I love the attention, I would trade anything to forget about life without you. In 1989, I was without you, as I am now.

OK, so maybe it's a stretch. And maybe a cigar is just a cigar. But I kind of like the retrospective hidden meaning. Are you laughing up there? Making fun of how I over-analyze everything. I miss your reassurance pep-talks whenever I'm in a tailspin of thinking too much and too hard. I miss those.

So maybe I skipped a number for no reason at all, and that's also a fine explanation. But I mean it when I say I don't like that year. 1989. A year without you. Just like 2019. My second full year without you. It just came to a close last night. And as I look into the future with optimism and a New Year's burst of motivation, I can't help but think, how every year, from here on out, will continue to be years without you.

NINETY-ONE.

I set out to write you one hundred letters, about all the ways I miss you, all the pains I hurt, all the words left unsaid. It's been an incredibly healing experience. I feel connected to you and more in tune with myself. I still see you and hear you and feel you, even though you've been gone for nearly two years. Two years? I feel like I blinked.

I don't think I'll ever run out of things to say. Even when I'm old and grey and sitting on some beachfront porch in a white wooden rocking chair, barefoot, sipping a midday mimosa (because that's the kind of 80-year-old I aspire to be)... even then, I'll wish you were there. I'll wish you were there to laugh with, to talk about our grandchildren, to reflect on all of the wonderful lifelong memories.

I will always wish you were here.

And as my hundredth letter comes creeping up to the finish line, I feel at a loss of words. How can I still have so much to say? How can I fit it all into just ten more letters. I think I've been creatively paralyzed at the thought of this task.

Eventually though, I realized, even a thousand more letters could never say enough. But that's love, you know. It's bigger than all the words and all the symbols this Earth has to offer. It's definitely much, much bigger than one hundred love letters.

So, as I continue to practice acceptance and the art of allowing. I'll repeat that I miss you, and I love you, and the world will never, ever be the same. I'll accept that you already understand my love on a level deeper than I'm able to, for now, as I continue to live this human experience. You already know. You didn't need these letters. I needed these letters. You already know that my love for you is eternal. I truly believe that.

So I'll say it again, and again, and again.... I'll never stop missing you. And that's OK.

NINETY-TWO.

Today, one of my close friends asked me about you. She's a newer friend, so you didn't get a chance to meet. She, and many others, have agreed to sign up for a 5K I am now a part of. We are going to run for you. She's never met you, but she'll be running for you. It's pretty amazing how far and wide the impact of a single person can spread.

She asked me about you today, and I delightfully paused and reflected. I thought of who you were. I was so appreciative to be asked about you. Too often people tiptoe around asking, afraid to offend or trigger me. Honestly, I love talking about you. You are woven into all of my memories.

You were kind, compassionate, oftentimes silly. You accomplished so much in a short life. You fell in love and had your heart broken. You owned your own business; built it from the ground up, and later sold it for profit.

You competed in fitness competitions and placed. You were the kind of friend that gave the shirt off his back. You were the kind of brother who called his big sister, just to say hi, and chatted for hours.

You travelled. Jumped off waterfalls in Hawaii. Road-tripped down the Baja California coast. Road dirt bikes in the dunes of Mexican deserts. Explored cliffs in the Caribbean.

I think about all of these aspects of you and what 27 years of Cody Anders gave to the world. I think about what your life meant to me and to all who knew you. I think about what your loss means to the world, and the domino effect it will continue to have. You made your mark, Code. I know that's all you ever wanted. To be seen, to be heard, to make an impact. You've absolutely made one.

I wish you were here to see it.

NINETY-THREE.

People have been commenting to me, friends and strangers alike, saying that they read my letters to you. Telling me how these letters make them feel, make them cry, make them think differently. It's honestly one of the most special things someone can say. "I've been following your posts and this is how it's impacted me." This is how you're changing the world, Code. How we are. Maybe in just small ways, but maybe big ways too. I like to think that you'd be proud.

Just recently a friend reached out to me, because of these letters, she felt safe and open. She told me about a family member who is struggling and I could hear her desperation to help. She asked for advice. "I'm no expert," I said. I hold on to the fact that if I were an expert, you'd still be here. Nevertheless, I listened to her and we shared our experiences. "Compassion," I told her. Compassion. If there is one thing that I could say, one piece of advice to give anyone struggling with addiction or who has a loved one who is in active addiction... compassion.

I look back on all the times I failed to give you compassion. The moments that I was unkind or frustrated. When I let my anger seep out. When I didn't understand the situation from an empathic lens, but took it personally. I told myself you didn't love me enough or else you'd stop using. I told myself you had a choice and you simply refused to make it. I regret those thoughts. I now see so clearly, and if I could go back in time, I would tell myself to have more compassion. That's it. No magic cure.

And maybe it would have still ended up this way, with me losing you. But, when I look back and remember the times when I did have compassion, I can truly say I did my best. It's that simple. That's the golden expert advice, just love them. Love yourself. This struggle is deeper than any choice or any decision. Substance use is a mask for soul-breaking pain. It's a coping strategy. And it works, until it doesn't. And when it doesn't, sometimes it's too late.

How can you not have compassion for someone who is simply trying so desperately to escape their overwhelming and painful reality. Haven't we all wished and begged for this escape.

Compassion.

NINETY-FOUR.

I sat down in my home office, the one I share with my husband. There was a card sitting on my side of the desk. "Don't ever give up on your dreams," it read. My first thought was that it was an old card I had written to him. I'm a handwritten card kind of girl. But then, I picked it up and opened it. I had written this card to you. For your 23rd birthday.

I yelled across the house to my husband, "Kris! Babe! Can you come here?" He approached and I asked him where he had found this card. He was confused. "I've never seen it before? Austin must have found it some-where." It didn't add up, but I accepted the explanation.

In the back of my mind, I knew you somehow had a hand in this little reminder.

I read the card, moved to tears. "You can always count on me.... I love you." I read the card a few more times.

There's a sadness to my words. There's a knowing that you're struggling. This card was given to you four and half years before you died. I was doing my best, from miles away, to let you know how much I loved you.

What if I actually did everything right? What if I truly did all that I could. This isn't the narrative I've been telling myself these past two years. But what if, just maybe, this is proof to the contrary. I did reach out. I hugged you. I loved you. I said all the right words. I jumped on planes and drove across town. I showed up when you called. Maybe I did more than I give myself credit for. And maybe this was just what was written in the stars.

What would it be like, I ask myself, if I were to change my narrative. If I were to forgive myself. And to forgive you.

NINETY-FIVE.

I woke up this morning and with my eyes still closed, placed my hand on my husband's arm, grounding into reality. I turned to him, a bit emotional, and said "I dreamt of Cody last night." It's always a mixed bag when I dream of you.

"What happened?" He asked. I was in a hotel, a very fancy hotel with gold-plated everything, and I was searching through the hotel, somewhat distressed. I was looking for my friends and couldn't find them. I walked down this fancy hallway where there was a bridge over a big pond, like one of those outdoor hotel lobby areas in Hawaii. I walked toward the elevator and I was waiting for it to open. Waiting for my turn to go up. I was sad to be alone, I couldn't find my friends and they weren't answering their phones.

As I was waiting for the elevator, I turned around, and Cody was there. I could see him clear as day. He looked really good, really healthy, really happy. He was smiling. He was wearing a very fancy suit. I was elated to see him. "Code!" I exclaimed. He told me that he was at work and he couldn't talk long but we could sit for a few minutes. We sat in these dark velvet chairs and talked. I asked him what he was doing here. He said he was head of security and that he was really happy. He had found his purpose, finally. He promised me that he was doing great. I didn't want him to leave, but I knew I had to get on the elevator to my floor.

I finished recalling my dream, I turned to Kris, and began to cry. "I miss him so much." I said, tears pouring down my cheeks and an audible whimper came from my cries. "I know you do, but he's head of security now." Kris replied.

I get it. You're head of security now. Thank you. I love you.

NINETY-SIX.

A funny, not so funny story: We paid thousands of dollars to a videography company to come and film our very small wedding ceremony. Thousands. And when they gave us the footage back, it was fucking awful. Yes, a proper use of a swear word. Dad said, "It looks like a drunk person was holding the camera." I was devastated and heartbroken. I demanded a full refund and the raw footage, to salvage some of it.

It's been over two years, and life got in the way a bit, but today Dad sent me a beautiful thirty minute video that he compiled together with the (tolerable) footage and the beautiful stills.

I found myself melting into tears as I watch you, alive and breathing; You held our rings during the blessing ceremony, and you held my hand in the photos.

This was the last weekend I saw you alive. You were far from well, but you mustered up the strength to put on a dapper suit and show up for me on this special day. You didn't complain. You showed with a smile. You drank alcohol-free champagne with me, and snuck me bites of your medium-rare steak because my pregnancy cravings forgot that I don't normally eat meat. We laughed.

I cherish the memories of that weekend. The time we spent together. I've been staring at a photo snapped from the video reel. We were holding hands, tightly squeezing. You can see the love in our eyes. A look that says, "I love you and I'm with you." That was always us. My heart aches with missing you.

NINETY-SEVEN.

I've been dreading writing you this one. I've been sitting with this information for nearly a month now. Just letting it weigh on my heart.

A few weeks ago, a friend of yours reached out to me. We messaged back and forth for over an hour. In the end he said, "I feel like Cody talked to you through me, to try and help you understand and feel better." Neither of us knew why now, why this Thursday night, did he feel so compelled to share the story with me. To share the story of your last day, of the hours leading up to your death.

He was there. He was your friend. He is an incredibly sweet man who also has had his struggles. He wrote me and said, "What do you want to know? I'll try to answer." I was shaking with emotion. All of my questions about what really happened that night were about to be answered. I felt blessed to be given answers, yet terrified to know the truth.

I asked everything. I asked where you were and why the rehab center wasn't supervising. Did you know what you were buying was pure Fentanyl. Why did you stop using the Suboxone after only a few weeks. Who was responsible? I asked why you were using alone in your room that night. Why didn't someone notice that you were under the influence. I asked every. single. question.

You didn't want to die, he assured me. He told me how you were neglected by the facility. How you were dope sick from no longer taking Suboxone. How you were at your absolute most vulnerable, and they were irresponsible. He said, "Cody was not weak. Anyone in the situation would have done the same. It wasn't his choice, it was like being in a fucking trance." He helped me understand who brought you to buy, and how you even said no at first. He explained that you used safely, with friends, until later that night when you used again. Alone. He walked me through his eyes that night, and the next morning.

I can't tell you how much I appreciate him. I thanked him. Knowing that your death was incredibly traumatic for him too. He told me that he felt guilty for not saving you. I told him I felt the same way. We bonded and connected over loving you and losing you. And now... now I know the truth about your last day.

NINETY-EIGHT.

I've loved writing you these letters. I've written more than a thousand letters in my head, all day long, when thoughts pop up, I speak to you. These are just the ones that have made it to paper. In many ways, it's been cathartic and connecting and so very helpful in my grief. In other ways, I'm just now realizing, it helps keep me at a distance. It keeps me as an observer of my experiences instead of an experiencer.

This grief is painful. It aches me and breaks me, deep down to my core. It's an enormity of sadness because of the enormity of love I feel for you.

I don't want this to be real. I don't want to mourn you and sit with the darkness of my grief. "It's unfair," I cry to the world. So incredibly unfair. But I know I just need feel it, and really truly feel it, so that I can get to the other side. Whatever is on the other side.

I think sometimes I resist the grief because to grieve you means you're truly gone. Gone from this Earth after nearly 28 years of being my brother, being my other half in so many of life's heartaches and joys.

But I know that I have to grieve you, over and over, day in and day out. Some days the pain is big and present, other days it's a soft whisper I barely notice. I'm learning to slowly accept this as my new reality, my new relationship with you.

I'll grieve you forever, until we meet again in the stars.

NINETY-NINE.

I spent the weekend in Northern California healing my heart on a meditation retreat. The set and setting were perfect. I felt so much love and nurturing in the space, with its wooden floors and giant windows, up in the Muir Woods.

Last night, deep in meditation, I had visions of you. I felt so profoundly connected to you. I was wearing my gold heart necklace, filled with your ashes, and found my hand placing over it again and again as I focused on my breath. "He is always with you," a voice in my head whispered, and for once, I truly believed it on a cellular level. Every day I continue to feel that love and the bond between us.

It's like I had a download from the Universe, from the stars, from the plants, from... wherever it is we all go. I became aware that you are finally safe. That you are no longer in pain. That you and Mom are in the same space. That somehow, someway, she is holding you again. This image brought me great joy, and relief. I choose to believe this as truth. She's holding you and you're back to being carefree and joyous in your new pain-free space.

I began to weep, feeling connected.

The mind is powerful. The breath is powerful. It allows us to move through energies and bring up great emotions. I needed this healing. I needed to sit with my grief, to let it rush through me, to cry, to be emotionally held, to dive into my consciousness.

I feel free. I feel lighter. I feel relief. "It was not your fault." That same voice retuned. This whole time, I was trying to find self-forgiveness for not saving you. I realize now that I don't need to forgive myself for something that wasn't my fault. And with that shift in thought, forgiveness came, compassion came, love grew.

I feel hopeful now, hopeful that the heaviness of my pain is lifting, and while I'll never, ever, ever stop missing you, I don't need to suffer. I know you're not suffering, either.

ONE HUNDRED.

Cody, you inspire me and motivate me. You fill me with pride and compassion. You live on in every breath I take.

May your life and your death never be in vain. May your story continue to reach others, and connect us all in love. It is connection that will eliminate shame and heal the world. Connection is the opposite of addiction.

I love you all ways, always. Across space and time.

Love, your big sister 🖤

Acceptance

Acceptance what a mouthful. What a heartful.

I feel pressure to write about acceptance and then tie it off with a bow. I am actively telling my mind to relieve myself of this pressure because a perfect closure will never exist. I realize that I may come to acceptance that my brother is gone but I will never be OK with it. Similarly, I miss my mother every day. I have wished she was here every single day since she passed on April 16, 2003. Every. Single. Day. I have learned that acceptance doesn't mean that you are OK with any of it.

Acceptance to me is the pause that comes after a deep inhale that fills your lungs and the deep exhale that follows. It's that moment of pause. Where you close your eyes and you nod your head to reality, as if you were saying, "OK. I concede. I accept this truth." It's incredibly painful, too, the path to acceptance, but once you are there,

there are moments of peace. I remember the first time I had a thought of acceptance; it was many, many months after Cody passed. I was outside, alone, in my hammock, staring up at the trees as the wind blew through them. *He's not in pain anymore.* I feel like I even whispered it out loud. Then I took that breath, nodded, and sat with this very comforting truth. Tears trickled down my cheeks in a soothing way, and I permitted my emotions to express. There was relief in this awareness. There was also some guilt for even allowing myself to be anything but angry and sad about this loss. The moment was fleeting, but it was a turning point in my grief. Slowly and infrequently, I would float into thoughts of acceptance.

I think if I was a religious person, I might have found acceptance more quickly. Perhaps I would have allowed myself the story that *he's in a better place*, as so many people told me in their poor attempts at comforting me. I suppose now I have warmed up to that phrase. A better place? It's hard for the scientist in me to believe this, but my spiritual heart continues to encourage me that it holds some truth. When I think about it, any place that he might be at is better than the immense pain and suffering he felt during his last years on Earth, when he was drowning in the darkness of addiction and disconnection. So yes, the "place" that he is currently in, it's a better one than that. I find some acceptance with these thoughts as well. Sometimes I think I confused acceptance with simply being accustomed to his absence. Now that two years have passed, my mind no longer automatically includes him in future plans. This breaks my heart immeasurably. I less frequently grab my phone to call or text him, wishing to share something only the two of us could understand. I even find that his name doesn't reach my lips as habitually as it once did, though I'm trying to continue to talk about him regularly. There's a sadness whenever I bring him up, even if I'm telling a funny story. All of this has been made possible with the passing of time. Perhaps these are signs of acceptance, or perhaps I am just used to it. I'm not sure how to truly tell the difference.

How will I ever accept something so unacceptable?

....

....

I hopped on a plane and flew to a land far away. A land unlike the one I live in. The commute was long, and I felt anxiety as I prepared for my trip. I found myself in a house, off the grid, away from it all, with nothing surrounding it but trees. I found myself in the presence of a medicine woman preparing me an herbal tea. This tea was unlike any other; it was made of a tropical vine and leaves of a plant. The tea was prepared for me deep in the jungle.

I had signed up to sit in a ceremony and drink spiritual medicine, a tradition of the Amazonian people. There is no limit to things you will do to ease your grief. This special plant medicine is known for its ability to heal the heart and speak to the soul. This medicine deeply affects the human consciousness. This medicine, I believe, can open your eyes to new perspectives and bring peace to a broken heart.

I sat in a small circle and listened as the medicine woman spoke. She told of the brew and of its magic. She assured a safe and loving container. She created a spiritual space where the drinker could heal. I remember the panic I felt rushing through my body. The mind creates a story of what the unknown could possibly be like. Fears and doubts and are quick to jump to the forefront. My hands were shaking, and I reached for the cup. I closed my eyes, whispering my intentions to the medicine. *Heal my heart. Please heal my grief.* I brought the shot-glass-sized cup to my lips and drank the brew. It tasted like nothing I could describe; it was gritty but had a thick consistency of molasses. It was not a pleasant flavor. I finished the cup, bowed my head to the shaman, and made my way back to my personalized area.

My area consisted of a cot, with blankets and pillows wrapped around me. I wore my gold heart necklace, filled with Cody's ashes. I held the necklace in-between my fingers. I lay down and closed my eyes. I breathed slowly, waiting for the effects of the medicine. They came on slowly, with a buzzing that started from the inside out. A warmth that built a fire inside. Then, with a few more breaths, I allowed myself to sink into a space of openness and receptivity. *I am willing to see what I need to be shown.* I decided in this moment to fully trust the medicine of the indigenous people, to not question the methods of this holistic healing. I kept my eyes closed for hours and allowed this special brew to take me on a journey through my consciousness.

Through the hours of my journey, I would hear Cody's voice. *I'm here, Nix.* It was if he was sitting right behind me. I wept. I screamed. I moaned in agony. I vomited up my grief and pain. I tossed and turned. I went on a rollercoaster ride through my emotions. "It was like a washing machine of fire," I told my husband upon my return. I felt guilt and shame and anger and rage. I had no choice, under the effects of the medicine, other than to sit with everything that came up and really feel it. There was no choice but to touch each raw emotion and to feel a rush of automatic thoughts and beliefs that came with it.

As a trauma therapist, I know that trauma needs to be recounted to be processed. When a trauma occurs, the brain does not have the capacity to store the memory properly. This is due to the effects of the fight–flight–freeze response in the autonomic nervous system. The trauma doesn't get coded properly and therefore it becomes stuck in your body. The best way to heal from trauma is to actually relive it. Not in the true sense of reliving it, of course, but in the sense that you need to reexperience the associated thoughts, feelings, and body sensations. You need to dive back into the experience, from start to finish, in a chronological and cohesive way. You need to expose yourself to all of it.

This is the magic of the medicine. The brewed tea has chemical effects on the mind that prevent you from having control over your thoughts and consciousness like you normally do. This blocks the mind from employing coping strategies like avoidance, repression, and distraction. You simply have no choice but to feel everything, all at once, even the darkest and most painful parts of your memory. It's equal parts terrifying and liberating. It is a tea for the brave among us who have true intentions of healing emotional wounds; this I can say firmly. I do not recommend an Amazonian journey for everyone, but for me this magic medicine was the experience that ignited the path toward acceptance. Through this medicine I found a way to feel what I was avoiding, and in that process, to see everything from a different perspective.

I believe the details of my specific psychedelic journey are best left for another memoir, but the outcome is what I am most compelled to share. I believe that there are many paths to healing, to this stage of grief where you begin to accept the awful fate of a world without your loved one. The most important factor of my experience with this Amazonian medicine was the ability that it gifted to feel my unfiltered feelings. The space to express without judgment. To revisit the memories in my mind that I thought were unbearable. This is the most vital step on the path toward acceptance—because how can you accept something you are unwilling to even think about or feel about?

....

....

What does acceptance look like, and how do I get there? I don't know the answer to any of it. I think back to the loss of my mother, seventeen years ago, and I ask myself, *Am I in acceptance?* I suppose the answer is yes. I'm used to it. My brain has rewired to understand that she is no longer here. My automatic urges to speak to her have subsided. I miss her, of course. I wish she could be here, to see my children grow. I think I actually miss her more, now that I have become a mother. I am able to understand her differently, appreciate her differently. Have I accepted that she is gone? Yes, I have. I don't cry myself to sleep about it anymore. I have integrated her loss into my story, into my identity. I've had 17 years to do this, and I think it took me most of them. The first time I even wrote about her death was on the five-year anniversary of losing her. For five years, I refused to write about it in my journal. I didn't want it to be real. Over time, I worked my way through that denial and into acceptance. It took a lot of sitting with myself, with my mind, with my heart. I just sat with my emotions and, bit by bit, healed.

That's what I am doing here, with Cody, with this new, very painful loss. I have only had a short time to process this, in comparison to the 17 years my mother has been gone. I'm not sure the timeline really matters much though. So why am I counting? Great healing can be done overnight, with an Amazonian brew, or a deep conversation. Or pain can persist for years and years, as someone refuses to look at it or experience it. I have worked with patients in my practice who, after fifty years, finally decide it's time to heal. There is no timeline. There is no normal. There is not direct route to healing and acceptance. I wish there was. I would write a step-by-step guide if I could, if only I could manualize it.

I believe the most useful aspect of moving toward acceptance is actually acceptance of the journey. Every day when you wake up, just feeling the emotions presented to you. Find ways to be present with the joy that comes, despite the heartache. Make time to be alone and really, truly weep. Move your body and allow yourself to express somatically and physically because our emotions are often nonverbal. Acceptance is about being OK with whatever shows up, trying not to fight it or change it. There is a technique called emotion surfing that I like to teach many patients. It has eight simple but powerful steps. 1) Notice your emotion. 2) Notice how it feels in your body. 3) Notice your thoughts. 4) Notice your behaviors. 5) Notice the intensity of the emotion. 6) Notice how the emotion peaked. 7) Notice how the emotion (thoughts, body, behavior) slowly diminishes over time. 8) Notice that you can handle it.

This emotion surfing technique is a simple reminder to purely **notice**. There are not instructions to fix, change, or alter in any way. There is nothing that would imply judgment or incorrectness. The guidance is just to notice.

This is acceptance. It's like saying, "Hello, emotion. I see you. I feel you. I am aware of your presence and how it impacts me. I welcome you as a part of my experience, even at your peak, for I know that you are merely a visitor who will come and go." This attitude helps me ride the wave of my emotions, even the very intense ones that take my breath away. This is how I find acceptance.

I miss my mom. I miss Cody. And...it just...is. That's my acceptance. It just is. I have learned that I can feel the grief and pain of loss while simultaneously feeling the joy and happiness that my life holds. There is no bow to tie at the end; no number of rituals or ceremonies or therapy sessions will bring them back or eliminate the grief of their absence. However, with enough work, I've been able to sit with and tolerate the emotions. They have softened in intensity and they do not define my story. I think this is what acceptance looks like. The ability to hold love and pain in the same breath. It is very common to be stuck in our traumas and feel defined by our losses.

For a very long time, I felt labeled as the girl whose mom died. I felt like it wasn't right to be happy because it in some way negated my pain or dishonored my loss. I felt that everyone I met needed to know that I was a motherless daughter, and in many ways, I acted as a victim of circumstance. It took me years to work through this and break free of the grief-chains that I encased myself in. It took me many years to come to a healthy acceptance of such a momentous loss. At times, I still weep for her, but I am not suffocated by the pain anymore.

It's been two years since losing Cody, and while I feel I am in the beginnings of acceptance, I am certain that the sporadic waves of sorrow will crash over me again and again. I am certain that I will continue to cycle through the jagged, nonlinear stages of grief. I do not have to end this book with a lie that I am perfectly healed. I have given myself permission to present my story as is. Unfinished and raw. I've done the work and will continue to do more work; I believe that is all anyone can do.

"Death has nothing to do with going away.
The sun sets.
The moon sets.
But they are not gone."
—Rumi

TWO YEARS.

Not unlike the first year, it's been a hard week leading up to April. Two years. Somehow it feels more painful. When you've done something once, it's novel. When you've done it a second time, it's routine. I routinely miss you. I habitually live without everything that made us NicoleAndCody; it was like one word growing up. Hitting the second year just reminds me there will be a third and fourth and so on.

More recently, I've managed to go a full day without thinking of you. I never thought it would be possible. An entire day without you on my mind. There haven't been many, but they've arrived. This fact isn't good, or bad, it just...is. We've all been talking about a new normal lately. The world is a bit crazy right now. There are so many memes I wish I could send you. So many heart to hearts and long conversations about conspiracy theories that we are missing out on. The world is cocooning, waiting for a new normal. It's just like grief.

The brain takes time to rewire to new norms. The heart takes even longer. We are all in this blurry phase; I know it all too well. Life without you has become my new normal, painstakingly. It only took me 731 days to say it.

I am thankful I spent this last year so intentional with my healing. Connecting to you through letters of love. I'm shifted; I'm dancing with acceptance. I feel the hole in my heart, but I've picked myself up and have begun to move on, move through, move forward. With only moderate kicking and screaming.

This next year, the third year without you. Will I ever stop counting? This year, I dedicate to connection. To big and bold gestures of love. To rising up from stigma and shame, all in your honor.

I miss you, Cody. I can't wait for the day when I no longer have to.

APPRECIATIONS

It is with such painful bittersweetness that I must acknowledge Cody's death as the catalyst to these writings. The sweetness comes when I allow myself to appreciate his life, the life we shared, and the immense love I feel for him, even in his absence. Without Cody, I would not be the woman I am today. He was one of my best friends; we were as close as any two siblings could be, even in our disagreements. Cody was my biggest cheerleader in life; he never hesitated to express how proud he was of me, and it always fueled me through. I only hope that he knew just how much he meant to me. Cody, I vow to continue to tell stories of us to my children and grandchildren. I vow to stand up against stigmas related to substance use and mental health. I will be the voice for us both, until I see you again.

To my wonderful husband, Kris, I thank you for your love. You have shown up for me in big ways and small. You are a safe space for me to land and a patient ear. I believe in the magic that brought us together. I am very thankful that you have walked hand in hand with me during our losses and our joys.

To my children: Austin Phoenix, you are my world sweet boy. You have healed my heart just by being you. You have been my biggest gift. From the moment I first saw you, I knew that I was born to be your mother. To my unborn baby boy, I cannot wait to hold you in my arms in a few short months. You have been a blessing to this family since the moment we found out about you.

To my mother, I miss you every day. If there is a Heaven like you so loyally believed in, I hope that you and Cody are finally together there. I hope that he is safe again in your loving arms.

To my father, thank you for doing what you always thought was the right thing. I know that you have made every decision with the best of intentions for your children. You are a good man, a great dad, and an even better Opa.

To Julie, my Madre, my second mother in this lifetime. Thank you for showing me unconditional love and support, even though you aren't obligated to. I believe my mother handpicked you from above and brought you into our lives. Thank you for being the best Nana to my baby boy.

To my siblings (Cody, Josh, and Dahlia) it is an honor to be your big sister. I love that we have such a big, blended family. I am so thankful for each of our close relationships. Thank you for being the best uncles and aunt to Austin.

To my best friends who have become family; you know who you are. Sometimes I look at my friends and think to myself, *How did I get so blessed to have this person to love?* You are my tribe and my heart. Thank you for listening to my grief, for showing up, for checking-in, and for loving me through all of it.

To Jordana and Yossi, two beautiful healers who have been a huge part of my journey. Thank you for your safe container, for your guidance in dark moments, and for the love and light that you give to the world.

To every teacher, therapist, and healer that has been a collective part of healing my heart.

To the vine of the soul, ayahuasca. Thank you for your perfect love.

To my yoga mat. Thank you for holding me, no matter how I showed up.

And lastly, but not at all least, to Jesse Krieger, my publisher. Thank you for being a wonderful roommate (except when we disagreed over the temperature), being my yoga accountability partner during the pandemic, and being a great friend who has shown nothing but support.

COVER ART

The cover art was designed with love by Dahlia Anders, Cody's little sister. Dahlia is a professional artist living in New York City. She is stylistically multifaceted and is proficient across all mediums.

For artistic inquiries: DahliaAnders@hotmail.com

INDEX

I mention several times that grief is not linear. Please do not listen to anyone who tells you otherwise. Your grief process is completely unique to you, and I urge you to be gentle with yourself. For me, I have felt days where every stage rips through me within minutes. Sometimes, I feel stuck for days in one particular stage. Right now, two years after losing Cody, I dance with acceptance. We are new dance partners, learning each other, finding a comfortable pacing and rhythm. And some days, I just don't want to dance.

These writings are chronological letters, and as you can see, I bounce from stage to stage. I hope that this shows you how normal it is to be nonlinear. I give you permission to embrace the chaos that comes with grief.

For posts on **ANGER**: 7, 9, 12, 17, 20, 28, 29, 31, 37, 46, 59, 60, 65, 66, 70, 71, 81, 90, 97

For posts on **BARGAINING**: 7, 11, 12, 20, 24, 27, 31, 33, 37, 43, 50, 57, 58, 64, 65, 66, 71, 76, 80, 87, 88, 93, 96, 97

For posts on **DEPRESSION**: 4, 13, 16, 19, 21, 22, 23, 35, 38, 39, 42, 46, 47, 51, 52, 57, 58, 61, 62, 67, 70, 72, 76, 77, 80, 83, 86, 87, 88, 89, 95, 96, 97, 98

For posts on **ACCEPTANCE**: 2, 3, 6, 15, 17, 18, 25, 26, 30, 32, 41, 44, 45, 49, 53, 54, 55, 56, 63, 67, 68, 73, 74, 75, 78, 79, 82, 84, 85, 86, 91, 92, 93, 94, 95, 98, 99, 100

ABOUT THE AUTHOR

Dr. Nicole Anders is a mother, wife, and big sister of five.

Dr. Anders is a licensed clinical psychologist. She specializes in treating PTSD and is trained in numerous evidence-based trauma-processing psychotherapies. Nicole believes strongly in the mind-body connection and, as a certified yoga instructor, finds ways to merge the worlds of psychology and yoga healing.

You can connect with her at **drnicoleanders.com** or on Instagram at *@CodysBigSister*

CPSIA information can be obtained
at www.ICGtesting.com
Printed in the USA
FSHW021412231120
76056FS